Paradise Regained
Fr. David Jones

Published by

MELROSE
BOOKS

An Imprint of Melrose Press Limited
St Thomas Place, Ely
Cambridgeshire
CB7 4GG, UK
www.melrosebooks.com

FIRST EDITION

Copyright © Fr. David Jones 2006

The Author asserts his moral right to
be identified as the author of this work

Cover designed by Bryan Carpenter

ISBN 1-905226-48-9

All rights reserved. No part of this publication may be reproduced, stored in a retrieval system, or transmitted, in any form or by any means electronic, mechanical , photocopying, recording or otherwise, without the prior permission of the publishers.

This book is sold subject to the condition that it shall not, by way of trade or otherwise, be lent, re-sold, hired out or otherwise circulated without the publisher's prior consent in any form of binding or cover other than that in which it is published and without a similar condition including this condition being imposed on the subsequent purchaser.

Printed and bound in Great Britain by:
Cromwell Press Ltd, Aintree Avenue, White Horse Business Park,
Trowbridge, Wiltshire, BA14 0XB, UK

To read is to be with a buried word
That could have lain unheard – to be alone
And not alone where memories are stirred
On this the page that stores them as its own:
'Tis to be all at listen, all an ear
Of inward hearing well, to answer not
But to be taught beneath a bygone year
By one whose mast'ry did not with him rot.
To write is to speak well without a voice
Across the years that threaten, 'tis to be
A little careful in a little choice
Of shapes that hold a sound that some may see
Tomorrow and tomorrow where we are
Not seen again, but heard afar, afar.

Introduction

"To know that I am Thine, and Thine shall be"

Probably in our computer age, with all the facilities of websites on the Internet and the unending round of poetry competitions, there are more poets, poetasters and would-be poets than ever before. There may well, however, be fewer that have gone to the pains of learning their craft than in former times. Dom David Jones, the Welsh monk, is not of this number. He has been writing steadily since the late 'seventies, and has emerged as a serious religious poet of considerable merit, who does not indulge in such sensational gambits as "having sex with God", which some contemporaries delude themselves is not only poetry but even "devout".

Born in Cardiff on 16 November 1953 to Welsh parents with considerable cultural interests, he was brought up in an ambience where religious practice played a considerable role in daily life. In 1967, in the lead-up to a Billy Graham summer campaign, he experienced an inner "conversion" and was baptised in the Baptist Chapel at Cardiff on 8 October 1967, assuming full membership of that community on 15 October. His indefatigable quest to know God was, however, only just beginning. Soon his reading convinced him that the truth in all its fulness lay with the Roman Catholic Church, but, owing to his youth, his parents and mentors advised him to wait awhile before seeking admission, though he already tended to attend mass rather than the services in the local Baptist chapel. On Holy Saturday, 10 April 1971, he was, however, "reconciled" to the Catholic Church by Dom Edmund Hatton (novice master), on behalf of his spiritual director, Dom Laurence Bénevot, in St. David's chapel in the crypt of Ampleforth Abbey.

After taking his A levels in the summer of 1972, he stayed on at school till Easter 1973, so that he might learn Greek. With impulsive generosity he immediately wished to enter Prinknash Abbey near Gloucester, a community of Benedictines of the Primitive Observance, who enjoyed a reputation for austerity. However, in view of his recent conversion and the fact that he had been awarded a scholarship for university studies, he was advised to take his degree first and went off to study Latin, Greek and Philosophy at the University College of Wales in Aberystwyth, where he graduated with joint honours in Latin and Greek in 1976. His monastic journey then began in earnest. After a stay at La Grande Trappe in Normandy, he made a retreat at the charterhouse of Sélignac near Bourg-en-Bresse before entering the Carthusian Order on 20 December 1976. It was at Sélignac that Dom David, as he was called in religion, began after a time to write poetry seriously, taking for his material his inner experiences in his search for the divine. If some echoes of Wordsworth, Coleridge and Hopkins are apparent, the monk at once found his own voice, and the reader is left in no doubt as regards the immediacy of the experiences depicted in 'The Threshold of Paradise'[1]. Eva Schmid-Mörwald, writing in the preface to 'Paradise Regained'[2], reveals her reaction to this first volume:

> 'When I first came across 'The Threshold of Paradise', a collection of verse written by a contemporary Welsh novice monk, I was stirred by the enthralling spirit radiating from the poems. The novice's love and reverence for the Creator were startling. Here a man was celebrating his love for God by creating poems of subtle beauty. His happiness was not unblemished though, for the road to perfection is a long and stony path, as was reflected in the verse. These poems grippingly captured the circumstances of their origin and whilst reading them I was bound to grasp some of the enormous inner tension that must have been present at their origin. I could feel the poet's urge to express his feelings and find an outlet for them. My interest was aroused: poet AND monk? The lines I had been reading were no feeble attempts in versifying, for they had a voice of their own; however, the two concepts of being both a monk true to heaven and a poet true to earth seemed to be too different to blend, particularly as it was the work of a Carthusian monk I had been reading. Wasn't that a contradiction in itself? Could these two vocations really be successfully united, sustaining each other in perfect symbiosis without

1 Anon., 'The Threshold of Paradise: The Poetic Journal of a Welsh Novice Monk', in *Analecta Cartusiana* 129 (1988), v-xii, 1-90. The volume was republished with a preface by the present writer and a blurb by Eva Schmid Mörwald as 'A Monk, The Threshold of Paradise', Adelphi Press, London 1994. Some of the poems were also reprinted in 'A Welsh Novice Monk, Poems Sacred and Profane', *Salzburg Studies in English Literature, Poetic Drama & Poetic Theory* 68:3 (1988), 5-45.

2 Anon. [A Welsh Novice Monk], 'Paradise Regained', *Salzburg Studies in English Literature, Poetic Drama & Poetic Theory* 146 (1996), iii.

doing harm to one another?

Brother David's monastic vocation is highly interwoven with his poetic vocation; there is a strong original link between his call to solitude and his urge to write poetry. For him the writing of poetry represents a means to praise his Creator but also serves as an outlet for accumulated feelings. The poet's urge to write is nurtured by his boundless belief in and love for God, the poems stem from the intensity of his religious experience. His first poetic volumes adopt the form of a diary, where we find poems as diary entries. They reflect the spiritual journey of their author in all its intensity and invite the reader to partake. Periods of unbound happiness and joy, when feeling the closeness to God, as well as times of appalling grief, disappointment and loneliness, when experiencing His absence, are captured in his verse, their honest straightforwardness leaving the reader dazed at times.'[3]

'The Threshold of Paradise' indeed mirrors the devotion of a Carthusian monk and his inner struggles, offering glimpses of an austerity unequalled by any other Catholic order. Unfortunately, the authorities of the Order felt — rightly or wrongly — that Dom David did not possess a purely Carthusian vocation, and, after his seven years of probation, he was not admitted to solemn vows, leaving the Order on 25 March 1984 on the expiration of his temporary vows.[4]

After a period of reflection, including retreats at Quarr Abbey and St. Hugh's Charterhouse near Horsham, Dom David decided to enter La Grande

3 In her blurb for Anon., 'Ad Maiestatem: The Journal of a Welsh Monk', *Salzburg Studies in English Literature, Poetic Drama & Poetic Theory* 146:2 (1997), she expresses similar sentiments: "His verse reflects the austere life in a Carthusian cell, mirroring a whole world which usually is firmly closed off from the rest of mankind outside the monastic walls. The firmness of his belief, assailed nevertheless by spiritual struggles, utmost despair as opposed to ecstatic happiness, the fruits of silence contrasted by desperate loneliness, represent an immensely fruitful source for his poetry ... his musings merge into a poetry not only of high spiritual value but also offer great æsthetic pleasure. The sonnet proves to be the poet's favourite verse form, a remarkable fact, as traditional verse forms, in particular such demanding ones as the sonnet, do not enjoy great popularity nowadays." Eva Schmid-Mörwald is also responsible for two major studies of Dom David's poetry: 'Poetry in the Order: A Welsh Novice Monk', in James Hogg, Karl Hubmayer, & Dorothea Steiner (eds.), 'English Language and Literature: Positions and Dispositions', *Salzburger Studien zur Anglistik und Amerikanistik* 16 (1990), 73-82, and 'The Lyre and the Cross in the Poetry of Alun Idris Jones', *Analecta Cartusiana* 129:2 (1994), a study containing detailed analyses of the poems and furnishing an excellent bibliography.

4 Dom Augustin Devaux, 'La Poésie Latine chez les Chartreux', *Analecta Cartusiana* 131 (1997), reveals, however, that a fair number of Carthusians did indulge in writing poetry. He devotes pp. 426-29 to Dom David Jones.

Trappe, a monastery that had always fascinated him. His volume 'A World within the World: The Poetic Journal of a Welsh Novice Monk'[5] reflects his experiences as a Cistercian monk of the Strict Observance, but here again his aspirations were disappointed, despite the undoubted seriousness of his intentions, which are clearly revealed in such poems as The twenty-fifth of March 1984.[6] The sonnet became his preferred verse-form for depicting his spiritual journey on the stony road to perfection. The chapter of La Grande Trappe held the opinion that writing poetry was irreconcilable with the Cistercian vocation, so, after nearly two years of trial, he moved on to the Trappist abbey of Roscrea in Southern Ireland, hoping to find the monks there more sympathetic to his poetic bent. Unfortunately for him Roscrea is unusual in running a school, which inevitably diminishes the seclusion of the monks to a certain extent. He struggled on for a time, but eventually left and returned to Wales on 20 June 1986. Far from being disillusioned, he was full of plans, contemplating becoming a recluse or even trying to re-establish monastic life in North Wales. At other moments he thought of engaging in the Charismatic Renewal in France. As no concrete possibility offered itself, he resumed studies at the Normal College in Bangor on 8 September 1986, obtaining a graduate diploma in primary education the following year.

The pull of the monastic life had by no means diminished, and he made retreats at a number of houses, before settling in for a prolonged stay at Ealing Abbey, a Benedictine house affiliated to the English Congregation in the suburbs of London. There he was advised to seek out a community more exclusively devoted to the contemplative life. Rather rashly, he chose Farnborough Abbey, not far from London, a house that had changed over from the Solesmes Congregation to that of Subiaco, but which somehow had never flourished. No doubt he was attracted by the musical tradition of the monks. He began his official postulancy there on 7 March 1988 and was clothed in the Benedictine habit on 10 December of that year, the Feast of St. John Roberts, taking the name of that saint.

The young novice did not find Farnborough as congenial as he had hoped. The community was small and passed through a dolorous crisis. Furthermore, the monks were heavily engaged in looking after the parish, which reduced the time available for a more strictly contemplative life. Early in 1989 he realized that he would not find fulfilment there and returned to Wales, where he resided at Talacre Abbey with Dom Basil Heath-Robinson, the former prior of Farnborough, for five weeks, pondering on the possibility

5 *Salzburg Studies in English Literature, Poetic Drama & Poetic Theory* 68:2 (1988).

6 Printed in 'The Threshold of Paradise', *Analecta Cartusiana*, 90.

of initiating a Benedictine foundation in North Wales. Though the Abbot of Ramsgate, Dom Gilbert Jones, was favourable to the venture, the local bishop was unsympathetic and withheld his approval. From April onwards the poet was enlisted on a project for translating the Church Fathers into modern English.[7] At the start of the new academic year, in the autumn of 1989, the poet enlisted for the Bachelor of Divinity course at University College, Bangor. Owing to his previous studies he was allowed to condense the three years into two, graduating in June 1991. Meanwhile he had been reflecting on the future. His spiritual director, Dr. John Ryan, O.M.I., felt that the Premonstratensian Order, with its ordered liturgy and tradition of study and prayer in community, might be the long-sought-for haven. He established contacts with Holy Trinity Abbey at Kilnacrott in County Cavan, Ireland. The poet entered this community on the Feast of St. Luke, 18 October 1991, and took the habit on the Feast of the Immaculate Conception, celebrated on 9 December that year. He reverted to the religious name Dom David.

After the first year of his novitiate he recommenced theological studies in Dublin. The volume 'A World beyond the World'[8] depicts his experiences at Farnborough, his time as a student at Bangor, and his novitiate at Kilnacrott. Inevitably, student life reveals different atmospherics to the daily round of the cloister, but his unalloyed joy at re-entering the religious life, where he might devote himself to God alone, is unmistakable. On 8 December 1993 he made his profession as a Premonstratensian. A few weeks later, on 30 January 1994, he was sent to study Spiritual Theology at the Angelicum in Rome, residing at the Premonstratensian house in the eternal city. He had learnt enough Italian in Dublin to get by, and as the canons at Kilnacrott engaged in pastoral and youth work, it was felt that such a course of study would be helpful to him in counselling work later.

At last, all seemed to have settled to a calm, which is reflected in his poems of the time, but further tempests were brewing up. Kilnacrott hit the headlines in the national press as a result of an unfortunate scandal. The superior was changed and even the future of the abbey seemed in jeopardy. Dom David was able to present his minor thesis in the early summer of 1995,[9] but was then ordered to return to Ireland. He obeyed, leaving Rome on 18 June, but, owing to the turmoil at the abbey, he requested six months'

7 This resulted in Oliver Davies, 'Promise of Good Things: The Apostolic Fathers', trans. Alun Idris Jones and ed. Oliver Davies, London 1992.

8 *Analecta Cartusiana* 129:3 (1993).

9 This has been printed as Br. David Jones, "Adam Scot: The tension in the psyche of the man of prayer between active and contemplative life", in 'The Mystical Tradition and the Carthusians', *Analecta Cartusiana* 130:11 (1996), 1-37.

leave of absence to reflect upon the situation. This was granted and Dom David resided for a time at Mount Tabor Hermitage in the west of Ireland, which had recently been consecrated by the Archbishop of Tuam. The solution could only be temporary, as he was not yet in Holy Orders, and therefore could not really act as chaplain.

That summer my wife and I had by chance visited the magnificent Romanesque abbey of Sant'Antimo, in a remote corner of Tuscany, where a small community, mainly from France, follow the Premonstratensian rule and sing the whole of the Office to the original Gregorian melodies in Latin in the abbey church. We were duly impressed, and, knowing of the crisis at Kilnacrott, we suggested to Dom David that this might be something for him. He duly arrived at the Abbazia near Castelnuovo dell'Abate on 6 December 1995, and though he hesitated to leave the official Premonstratensian Order for some weeks, as several poems in the present volume reveal,[10] he finally decided to join the community at Sant'Antimo, where he made his solemn profession on 9 December 1996, and was ordained to the priesthood in Siena's beautiful medieval cathedral on 31 October 1997. Soon thereafter he returned to the Angelicum, where he presented a doctoral thesis of the highest distinction in December 1998.[11] He now occupies the combined posts of sacristan and guest-master at Sant'Antimo, and since March 2000 has also been given charge of the noviciate.

Some poems from this period were printed in 'Ad Maiestatem',[12] but this new collection gives a much more detailed overall picture of the poet's spiritual pilgrimage from the time of his first studies in Rome up to his reclothing in the Premonstratensian habit which, under dramatic circumstances, he had to shed. A much greater tranquillity is immediately apparent, even if some longings remain unsatisfied. As in previous volumes, the poet shows himself to be an expert linguist, writing with equal facility in Welsh, English, French, Italian, Latin and Greek. There are no poems as yet in German, though there are several German headings, and after residences at Wilten Abbey near Innsbruck and with the Benedictines in Augsburg to learn the language, it only seems a matter of time before he tries his hand in that language too. Dom David is not an avant-garde poet. In some respects the poems in the slim volume recently issued for a monk of Parkminster are more "modern" in their texture, but the slightly archaic tone on occasion has

10 Cf. particularly the poem *Rome*.

11 Printed as Br. David Jones, 'An Early Witness to the Nature of the Canonical Order in the Twelfth Century: A Study in the Life and Writings of Adam Scot, with Particular Reference to his Understanding of the Rule of St. Augustine', *Analecta Cartusiana* 151 (1999).

12 Several poems are reprinted in the present volume.

been deliberately chosen as appropriate to clothe the religious content. The topics are almost exclusively concerned with the daily round of the religious life, and we see the poet learning to say the mass, listen to his innermost thoughts about his profession and ordination, his joy in celebrating the mass in abbeys and churches that had meant much to him in the past, his administering the sacraments and preaching retreats, even as far away as at a nunnery in Rumania, his enthusiasm for pilgrimages, such as Medugorje, which the present writer has always felt rather reserved about, as also for Dom David's enthusiasm for miracles, wonders and signs.[13] Even after his ordination, he was still dreaming of restoring the monastic life in Wales, as *Penmon* reveals, and his fascination with the solitary life as led by the Carthusian and Camaldolese Orders remained, as we see in *This is the day*, *A New Reverend Father*, *Chartreuse*, *Letter from the Grande Chartreuse*, *Unopened*, *Eve of Saint Romuald*, *Recluso*, *Eremo*, *Dom Damien*[14], *Reading lines penned beside Dom Damien's tomb*, *Haunted*, and *Letter to a friend.*

13 This enthusiasm was apparent in earlier volumes of verse and in Alun Idris Jones, 'The Purgatory Manuscript. Le Manuscrit du Purgatoire', *Studies in Women and Religion* 29, Lewiston, N.Y. 1990.

14 Dom Damien had been a Carthusian at Sélignac, but he transferred to Camaldoli and died as a recluse there.

It may be significant that, despite its French title,[15] he chose to write his profession poem in Welsh. However, there are poems in English revealing the depths of his feelings about his profession and ordination, which cannot fail to move the reader:

Vous avez été accepté

(à l'unanimité)

O! joy on earth! O! joy yet in the world!
To know that I am Thine, and Thine shall be,
And Thine alone, and by a little word
Upon this altar placed, eternally
To this Thy temple joined — to know that now
No man or angel fiend can mar the road
Trod here by friends now crowned, that once did bow
Here where I place my head: to see the cloud
Of witnesses unseen walk calmly by
And chuckle at an æon, to see all
Melt in a moment felt, nay, and to cry
A tear of blissful peace — this is to call
From out of the abyss of Failure vast,
And clutch at but a notch of grace at last:

or:

15 *Vous ferez la profession le neuf décembre*, reflecting the Prior's own words.

In petram inaccessam mihi deduc me

O joy! I shall yet hold Thee in my hand
Upon this ancient stone where others felt
The passing of their God: I shall there stand
Where souls have stood before and angels knelt
At veilèd Mystery — I see the light
Of Tabor in this night, for this one word
Of manhood made is weighed with Godhead's might,
And in one chrismic sound I have all heard.
O Master of this astral path we tread,
I hear, I hear the voice that never was
By mortals caught, and here my little head
I bow to Thy great blessing: this day has
A ray of touch electric hither sent,
And o'er a sound the heavy cosmos bent.

or:

How beautiful are the feet of those who bear *good tidings*[16]

O! bliss in but a sound! O! happy day,
That changes every day for evermore,
That brings back yesterday from far away,
And sparkles with a grace once known before!
A word this hour was heard that has a pow'r
Beyond the noise of scribblings and of hands
Not driven from above; nay, one small hour
O'er years of heavy waiting calmly stands.
My God, I shall Thee touch, I shall Thee hold,
And be Thy voice on earth — I shall be free
To climb these ancient steps and there be bold
To walk alone 'mid clouded Trinity.
I shall, hid Friend, for ever and a day,
A Priest be, till the æons fade away.

16 Prior's news of Dom David's ordination ("C'est un des jours les plus heureux de ma vie!").

Less exclusively autobiographical, and therefore applicable to us all in these days of super-activism, is:

What is this life?[17]

There is too much to do on earth, and more
Than need be done is done by all that do
Too much to do all well, for this one law
Of patient moments old, that ancients knew,
The new-found sound of man can ill contain,
And waning is the moon that should have known
To slowly be, to wholly be again
What once it calmly was to days outblown.
O Master of the energies of flesh,
That twitch and chatter o'er a loudest day
That held a bulging load, what did enmesh
The very brain that breathed, till it should pay
A debt too heavy to a great machine
That had no pow'r to stop till all had been?

The present volume not only offers a graphic portrayal of the pilgrimage of a soul willingly and unreservedly placed in God's hands in often arrestingly beautiful poetic diction, but also exudes much sane wisdom, from which the modern reader, whatever his religious commitment or lack of it, can profit.

Ash Wednesday 2000 James Hogg
University of Salzburg

17 A Carthusian's words: J'ai gaspillé... ("I have wasted my life doing too many things").

Au lecteur

Take not too much, my friend, of this delight
That will to souring turn: take but a sip,
A little in the dying of the light
That was thy rousèd day, for on the lip
A word caressed is blessed more sweetly when
'Tis heard alone and left alone to stand,
And where the words of many hurried men
Cry oft there is no softness in our land.
My friend, hear well, and this the bell that comes
Again, again, to call a hermit home
Will travel too to thee, and what becomes
Tomorrow here today will onward roam
There where thou art, within, deep, deep within,
If thou wilt halt a sound, and enter in.

Guardians

(We asked Jesus, through a child, the names of our guardian angels, and thought it would be good to honour them with verses.)

Rita

Unseen and hidden friend, walk by my side,
And guide my feet;
Teach me to turn to thee, in thee confide,
And thee entreat,
For thou art there, and thou dost care for me,
And dost but ask
That I at times thee greet.

Paul

Unknown and loving guest that hovers high,
Guard, keep and guide my steps, for here below
We do not see as we are seen on high,
And need at times a friend the way to show.

Catherine

My little friend, whom I see not, but know
To be at hand,
Watch, keep and guard my footsteps as I go,
And by me stand,
For I am small and can but call thy name,
And in this land
Thy wing the way must show.

My little friend, be with me to the end,
And love me well,
For I am thine, all thine – and so defend
From pow'rs of Hell
This tiny one that cannot walk alone –
For thou canst tell
What unborn hours will send.

My little friend, another day will come,
Another go,
And after all our days another home
Will one day show
The fairness of thy hidden face to me
Who cannot know
What worlds thy feet now roam.

John – mon ange

Ami inconnu, connu par les cieux
Que tu habites, guide-moi ce jour
Vers demain, vers le demain de mon Dieu,
Car hier manqué manquera toujours.

(Mélodie: Rhys)

Guardians: Written after we had experienced their quasi-miraculous intervention upon invoking them.

26 August 1993

Et Verbum caro factum est

O Geidwad mwyn, a droediaist hyn o fyd
Am awr neu ddwy
O blith yr hen eonau sydd o hyd
Yn teithio drwy
Bellteroedd ac amseroedd gynt a ddaeth
Oddi ar dy law,
Dy orig heibio aeth.

Cans rhannu wnaethost rai eiliadau crai
O'n dynol rod,
A gwisgo wnaethost hyn o henaidd glai
Sy'n cynnal bod
Y pethau bychain hyn na fynnit droi
Yn ôl, yn ôl
I'r fan lle mynnent ffoi.

Ac y mae heno yn nistawrwydd hen
Yr aros maith
Ryw wybod am ryw hoff gyfarwydd wên
A gofia daith
I gornel o'r mesurau na all gloi
Y cyfan sydd
Yn dal am byth i droi.

Oherwydd ynot Ti, anwylaf Un,
A wylaist dro
Ym mröydd dagrau, lle y troedia Dyn
Ar greulon gro,
Fe welwn wawl y Cread nad yw'n bod
Ond ynot Ti,
Fu'n mesur echdoe'i rod.

The Sacred Head

O Sacred Head, that held the Godhead's mind,
And thought of us,
While bearing here the weight of human kind
And gazing thus
Upon the æons thus to come and go,
Look here awhile,
And bid us thy thought know.

O little Head, that read the thoughts of Earth
Without a word,
Place here thy pain, and while the world's dark mírth
On high is heard,
Rest, rest a little while thy piercèd brow
Upon our own,
That we thy thought may know.

O tiny ball, whose call the spheres had heard,
And come to be,
Hold all the thought of thinking in a word,
And quietly
Perceive the grieving of the soul too slow
To pause, to pause,
Thy thought awhile to know.

O mind of Christ, the kindness of all care
E'er shed on Earth,
Beam into us a knowing of what there
Is of true worth,
Ere in our haste we marvel as we grow,
At many things,
And fail thy thought to know.

Mary

From thorns a drop of honey forth did run;
From darkest cloud the morn-star beamed as sun,
And yet of thorns the drop bore not a taste,
And cloudedness the star knew not – 'twas chased:
For drop and star, of such strange origin,
Such gentle and sweet rising, Virgin-bright,
Were but a light to figure what would be.

(The ancient Latin original runs as follows:

Mellis stilla de spinis exiit,
Maris stella de nube prodiit – tenebrosa,
Sed spinosum nil stilla sapuit,
Sed nubosum nil stella habuit – radiosa:
Stilla, stella talis origine
Dulcis ortus et clara Virginis – sunt figura.)

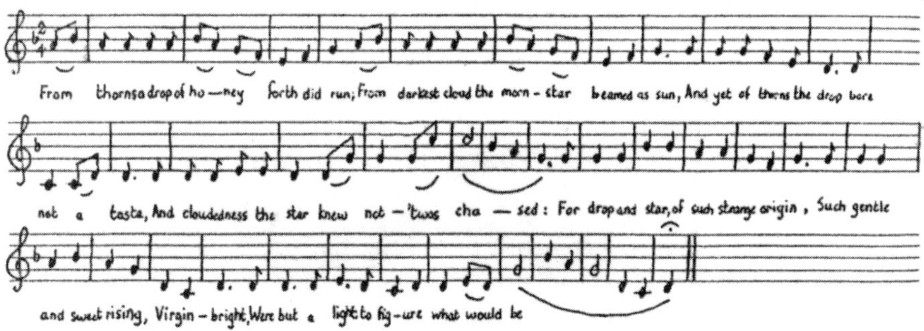

Resta con noi

Bydd gyda ni, O Geidwad, yr awr hon;
Bydd gyda ni, arho in dy hedd.

(Cytgan:)

Aros yn awr, heb ymbellhau:
Ni fydd hithau'r nos iti'n nos.
Bydd gyda ni, cadw ein traed
Ar hyd lwybrau ein bywyd drwy'n hoes.

Fe'th ddygwn Di at bob un o'th frodyr:
Geiriau o'th Air fo adlais Dy Lais.

(Cytgan:)

Aros yn awr, etc.

Rhoddaf i Ti fy nwylo, fy oriau:
Rhoddaf i Ti fy nghalon, fy oll.

(Cytgan:)

Aros yn awr, etc.

Be with us now, O Lord, as it darkens;
Be with us now, and we shall be safe.

(Chorus:)

Be with us, Lord; walk at our side:
The night nevermore shall come down.
Walk with us now, and here abide,
For the world that we tread is Your own.

We shall bear You to all these Your brethren;
We shall bring You along every path.

(Chorus:)

Be with us, etc.

Here are our hands, our feet, and our moments;
Here evermore are our hearts: all is Yours.

(Chorus:)

Be with us, etc.

18 May 1994
(Rome)

The picture in the Bible

There was an odour which would fill the world
With memories of hoping: there was bliss
Within a second wherein hours were hurled
From days of hurting ecstasy – for this,
My dream, was all of thee in mystic form,
And in two nostrils particles of pow'r
Could jerk the nerves within till they did storm
The dormant depths of Memory's lost hour.
O! wanted one, that wanted to be one
An hour or two with all the time to be
Engraved in cervic banks, a work is done
That undone ne'er shall be – for though I see
But papered smiles, there is awhile within
A fondness in a paradise so thin.

22/5
(Pentecost)

Unless you change, you will not be received for Solemn vows

(Abbot's words regarding solitariness)

To be alone beyond the world of sense
Or to be sensed by all that sense can own;
To be upon a lonely shore all dense
With absence vast and Presence only known,
Or to be held and felt, to feel a hold
Of old familiar fondling; to be owned
And warmed in one small corner of the cold
And frightened cosmos, or to be yet crowned
With hurting martyr's pricks – for these words come
Not from a heart whence we can not be lost –
This is the choice, for now the voice of Home
Is long since never heard; for though 'tis crossed,
The Rubicon still flows, and knows the way
To bring us back again to yesterday.

A lonely shore: the shore of the Atlantic, at Mount Tabor Hermitage, whose foundress had urged me to think of it.

Unattended moments

They will not come again from whence they stood
Once o'er heads unheld – they will not come
To roam unhurried where the worried blood
Found not a time to pause, for Duty numb
Had hardened every vein: no more, no more
Will seconds have a second time to be
A part of us, nor can this little core
Of being that we are be history.
A moment glowed – of troubled ecstasy,
For that 'twas hardly known, nay, was outblown
For hurry for the next – yet next we see
That it itself was best, it, it alone.
And it asunder breaks the selfsame heart
That beat it once, not knowing beating's art.

Vacans

Alone with but the word and all the sound
Of Silence – nay, alone and home again
With truth of naked knowing, be it bound
'Twixt covers of live volumes, be it plain
To see and hear within, where nothing mars
The clarity of seeing, hearing all
And touching all that moves beyond the bars
Of soft recluded sensing – voices call
Across the quietness that can alone
Hear something gently stir, for blurring not
The faintest sense of all, we sense all groan
With resonance unheard or long forgot.
O Master of the Dark, I see no more,
And yet I think I have walked here before.

A true nun

(Sr. Arpana's kind present)

Nay, many angels walk this earth unseen,
And we see not the wings on which they fly
Without a noise to where, 'tis said, have been
These souls that are our spark – for once on high
At th'instant of our being, He did beam
His image in our soul, and for a while,
A while as small as nothing, it would seem
That we were giv'n to see that ancient Smile.
O! little ones that fill another world
Not often worth a thought, think on these things
That matter unto some, and let your word
Remain as hid as you, for even wings
At times were lost by some who thought too much
Of where they flew, for flight was never such.

Lines written near the tombs of Keats and Shelley

To leave a word that will be heard awhile
When we have ceased to be – to be beyond
The shore of this wide world, and yet beguile
The thieving death-moth and the eerie wand
That struck ere pen had gleaned the teeming brain:
To stand, stand very still where stillness stands
Against the rush of passing, and again
Be heard without a voice, but only hands –
This is to halt a second in its course
And bid it hold an æon: 'tis to call
The unknown passer by to intercourse
Of soul with lying soul that has said all.
This is, my friend, to hold on to the end
Of Youth and Beauty that no time can mend.

Feeling

Beyond the veil what is there to be seen,
What heard in this huge realm of silence long –
And thou, good pilgrim, who that way hast been
And comest back this day to tell thy song,
What didst thou find? And what is left behind
Here where we wander still, does it bear thought –
Nay, canst thou think of this, or are souls blind
To what is to the sundered body wrought?
Walk on upon a cloud, our unknown friend,
And wear this badge that men on angels pin,
For though we do with great devotion bend
O'er thy roused bones, we cannot enter in
To fields of vision that these sockets see,
Or palp the body of an ecstasy.

Bones: Today the coffin of a former Grand Master was opened, for examination regarding incorruption, in preparation for beatification.

[קֹהֶלֶת]

There is a time to be together well,
A time not so to be – a time no more
In mingling to be poured; there is a time to swell
The heart with growing yearning at hope's door,
A time to yearn no more, and to be still
To hear the echo of an ancient word;
A time again to ponder 'neath the thrill
Of unarousèd bliss in something stirred.
For there's a time when hearing comes anew
Through ears and eyes and all that opened is
To its own hour, for Time is only true
To one alone: the one that is all his,
For many times are wanted by the one
Who knew not th'hour of each thing 'neath the sun.

A night

Will this yet be, O Light, will this yet be,
That Thou didst in a vision give to one
On that fair em'rald isle? Canst Thou now see
Tomorrow as today, and does the sun
That sleeps awhile as we but toss and turn
Arise upon a morrow Thou hast known?
For in the night I feel a something burn,
And in the flame a name not fully blown.
For many fires yet glow in deepest dark,
And some walk no more on, once known these sighs.
Yet can I yet forget this little spark
That flashed and flashed as that saint closed his eyes?
He saw the shape of Erin, and it seemed
That o'er the North a little novice beamed.

News

(By the time you receive this letter it will be published)

The power of ink can bend the heavy years
And draw a smile from Reason – e'en the sight
Of carvèd sounds can stroke the hurting fears
Of knowing not the outcome of the night.
Nay, I perceive that strokes can stroke our all,
That there is here, within vibrating lines,
A flow of something mighty e'er so small
That it can touch the untouched part that pines.
I knew not what would come, I knew not well
The world that lay beyond the homely wall
Of solitude's soft pain – I loved the hell
Of wanting and of yearning for the all
That had been left behind, and here I find
The hours of hurting trapped in th'ages' mind.

Gregorian

There is a beauty in the heav'ns that here
The earth has ever heard whene'er this came
From something in its soul, for ancient fear
At all the weight of Being e'er the same
Was felt, is felt, and will be felt with this
The sound of human sadness, and the years
That travel on these lines that hold the bliss
Of Melody all sensate stroke the ears –
Not of a tympan's tremble, but of all
That moves at something fair there where we are
Within, within, awakened by a call
Sent by a fellow-pilgrim from afar.
For he cries out across æonic sound
Of some deep, deeper realm of music found.

Maggio

An angel is not clad, and there is air
Enough for him to move on agile wing
With all the speed of thought, and, wholly bare,
He patters at the Throne and yet doth cling
To his own little ward who 'neath his gaze
Would be as white as he – for in the light
Of this our ancient way we tread the days
And hours canonical 'mid Song's delight.
And yet upon a heat of Latin day
A classic ray of mischief can yet beam,
And there is 'neath an angel's habit play
With pleasing lightness of a passing dream.
For airy is the hour when something moves
The all of one whom noon and demon proves.

Flicker

To stand before the Altar and to call
Not sounds, but Him the Word – to stand and bow
Before a Godhead e'er so very small
That He might fain be missed, for all the how
Of Heaven's mighty move at this strange sound
Was by no engine traced, and mystery
Is best in silence drawn, for more is found
In incense dense than in philosophy.
O! wonderment of Pulling all unseen:
What is it thus that magically moves
The deepest depths of Man from 'neath this screen
Of Shekinah all veiled? Nay, what are loves,
When Love itself in gentle glow doth say,
Wilt thou, my friend, my friend, too go away?

Here

What is it, Master, what is lying here?
What is the essence of a presence hid?
I cannot know, yet know there's something near,
Nor hear, yet hear within a something bid,
"Come close, come closer still, come very close –
Nay, thou'rt not close enough, for two need be
Not very far apart." – For one small dose
Of magic from a God works heavily.
O thinker of all Love, tap gently on,
And draw where Thou art drawing, for alone
I can but love the fair, and where there's none
But fairness dark, I love a light unknown.
For though I see Thee not, I touch Thee well,
And there is looking in a little cell.

Noise

The air is seldom clear, and many things
Hit hard upon the ear, that cannot be
But open and alert, for thoughts have wings,
And some mouths bid all fly, as 'twere as free
In going as in coming to the mind,
The very pulse of chatter yet we need
Not to say much, for such when left behind
Can matter more if we the Matter heed.
For nothing matters more when more is said
Than need be let to cloud the virgin sky,
And I recall how once my ears were fed
With but a little whisper and a sigh,
That did bid nothing say but only be,
And in the darkened list'ning something see.

Pourquoi?

(Pourquoi as-tu voulu être prêtre? – Florencia)

Un angelet qui passe et ne vient plus
Sur nos chemins; un ange, dis-je, qui
Sourit un jour et reste aussi connu
Que toutes les inconnues d'aujourd'hui
Qui demain n'auront pas un souvenir
Dans mon esprit – un ange qui s'envole
Vers ces espaces de bel Avenir
Qui passe déjà et déjà nous vole . . .
Ô petit rien du tout, ô petit monde
Qu'inondera sans doute un univers
D'avènements trop brefs, si je te sonde,
Où trouverai-je un écho á ces vers?
Et quand au soir tu auras tout connu,
Sauras-tu reconnaître l'Inconnu?

9/7
(Université d'Innsbruck)

Hier ruht in Gott...

Geb. am 16.11.15
Gest. am 26.4.92

We come and go, and no one knows the way
But they that come no more; we here are born
Upon a day our own, and on a day
The twain that danced awhile, asunder torn,
Take paths their own, and shift into a land
That, clutching, they'll not tread, for here alone
The ghostly must be all, and not a hand
May touch the being 'neath this heavy stone.
O little home, of flow'rs so deftly tucked
As though a bed for sleep, could we peep in
And in and in to where the soul was plucked
From its familiar half, what unheard din
Would travel from the hush of this deep tomb
Where moves no more what moved into the womb?

10/7
(Wilten Abbey, sitting beside a grave)

16.11: my birthday also.

Mo

Mae engyl eto'n troedio yma a thraw
Ar lwybrau cudd y byd; y mae rhyw rai
Na welir gan fawr neb, ond eto daw
I'm meddwl bach, a welodd yn ei wae
Pa gysur a pha bleser driphlyg fawr
A gerddai lonydd hoff fy henwlad fwyn,
Ryw ergyd na all fod, cans gwn yn awr
Fod wyneb doe ryw ddolur heddiw'n dwyn.
O dyner un, pe gwyddwn am dy boen,
A'th angen am na fydd – pe gwyddwn gynt,
A gefnwn ar dy wedd lle dawnsiai hoen
A gwên nad oedd mo'i thebyg yn y gwynt?
Ond, dawel angel Nef, a wyddost ti
Fod Arall yn dy garu'n fwy na fi?

18/7
(Abaty Wilten)

Mo: "She should be a nun." (Jesus' reply regarding Maureen, through a child.)

Yn ôl

Y mae i'r galon ddolur nas gwêl un
Ond ef a'i dwg, ac nid oes le i ddau
O fewn yr enaid caeth, yr enaid sy'n
Ymguddied yn y fron, lle'n awr y mae
Y pethau nad ŷnt mwy, yn dal i fod,
Yn dal yn rhan o'r byd lle buont gynt
Yn wir un awr – yr awr sydd eto'n dod
Yn ddidrugaredd ar adroddus hynt.
Pa bethau fu ers imi fod fan hyn
O'r blaen – pa bethau ffôl a dynnodd oll
O'm gafael, gan fy ngadael heddiw'n syn
Yng nghwmni'r doe a'r echdoe sydd yngholl?
Cans cwmni sydd i'r enaid, cwmni prudd,
Ac nid oes un a'n gwêl, cans rŷm ynghudd.

13/8
(Cymru)

Sitting in the old place in the library

Three years have passed and more – and more has been
Than e'er I thought could be, since I sat here
And cast before upon the page the spleen
Of worried Youth, and travelled very near
To utterness of Bliss and very Hell
When matters grew too large and here again
I heard the distant call, the unheard bell
That did chime on and on above Heat's pain.
O passing of an æon! What are we
That hurt a little while till we no more
Have pow'r to hurt, or any more to be
But memories of something gone before
Into the chasm of a void so great
That none will ever know what filled its weight?

19/8
(Bangor)

Rhyferthwy

Pa beth yw hyn; pa beth, fy Nuw, yw hyn
Sy'n tynnu yma a thraw, sy'n rhwygo'n ddwy
Y galon na all ddal yr hyn a fynn
Yn dawel fel o'r blaen, cans bellach mwy
Sy'n llifo dan y fron nag unwaith fu,
Ac y mae gormod grym yn llenwi llon
Â hoffter am gyfarwydd bethau cu
Sy'n dawnsio yn fy nghof â'u llygaid llon.
O! boen! O! olaf hoen a allsai fod
Yn bopeth am un dydd! A fyddi di,
Fy angel cudd, a fynnaist rywsut ddod
Yn hysbys yr awr hon, ein horig ni,
Yn ddim ond rhith i'r cof, yn ddof dy rym,
Ynteu yn fwy na mi, a minnau'n ddim?

25/8
(en retraite, Gort Mhuire)

Miracle

(on photograph)

Wouldst thou, good Mother, have me hear a sound
Upon this quiet sheet – a sound to pierce
The sadness of the darkness where is bound
The heart now torn apart by tugs so fierce
That something fiercer still must pull along
To where thou'st have me go? O gentle Maid
That dost feign here to weep, with sighs so strong
That e'en their pain is seen in blood unmade,
Dost thou behold, in holding near thy breast
The Sun of Justice that thy womb did bear,
That some small mighty demon here did nest
Within the pangs of Wanting that did tear
Away from what within a while could be
If I by one blind sheet be made to see?

30/8
(en cellule)

Photograph: "It is our miracle!" (The Sacred Host has appeared over the Immaculate Heart in one of the two pictures that Ellen took of the statue weeping blood.)

The prostitutes

O! lonely ones who walk with many men
Into a heat so cold that naught can melt
Or touch or reach aught in the hidden den
Of hard iniquity of hearts unfelt
Amid the feel of all – O! little ones
Much used to fill with streams of unthought sense
Where truth with gesture copulated runs
No more, and nearness holds a distance dense, –
Where do you lie when you must lie alone
With thoughts unpierced, with moments not yet sold
To gazes all of greed that feed a stone,
Again, again in this familiar hold,
And do you feel when held by oft a clutch
For but a little meaning in a touch?

15/10
(Rome)

Violence enveloped

When in a thin-walled space a face is hid,
There can be joy in molecules of ink,
And when a page in rage doth now forbid
The heart to smile, but would have it e'er sink
Into a slough of hugely black Despond,
There is a moment when momentous things
Vibrate between two ears, and when the wand
Made of a tiny Nay vast magic brings.
Nay, nay, 'twas not for hate that we were made,
Nor was there merit in an unsaid prayer;
Nay, neither was the Truth of foul sound prayed,
Or Beauty worshipped in a starkness bare.
I see not well into the night ahead,
But e'en the dark I fear less than the dead.

Mysterium tremendum et fascinans

Will there be in a place a space for us
To be alone with love, to be alone
For loving in a beauty offered thus
To Thee its origin? Is this outgrown,
The oddness of a pain to gain a bliss
Made of a heavy harmony, a sound
Not made of unthought whistling, but of this
The work of years and years that something found?
Nay, we have found too quickly what a cloud
Of wonder hid for long; we have climbed up
The steps of Godhead with a coldness proud
To be so close to this plain bread and cup.
O! Awe that made us all, I am not sure
That I can see all shove Thee, and endure.

A bad name

To own a name that is not mine to own,
And be well tarred with sins ne'er even thought;
To be a part of darkness clearly shown
By one small lighthouse that the eyes hath caught
Of all upon this isle – to be, for e'er to be
Not what I am – this is not to be all
That I can be, for though 'tis night I see
A twinkle in the dark, and hear a call.
O Master, 'tis to Thee that I have vowed,
And, vowing, giv'n my all, and Thine own Hand,
That held my promised moments as they flowed
Upon the sacred sheet, may yet withstand
A tragedy too great for human kind,
For e'en a vow to Godhead God can mind.

28/10

Enquiry

O Archipelago of distant isles,
All waiting for a word, what word will come
From one who holds the magic of these miles
Of tranquil and of hung'ring home and home
In separated homesteads – what lies 'yond
The ancient barrier of the hills and waves
Whence few return to places once so fond,
And whose long moments none unthinking braves?
O land whereon a question mark stands writ,
Art thou to be a warmth from this great cold
Far colder than the North, and do I sit
Before a page that, though a little bold,
Can hold the door of freedom at a turn,
And many, many errors yet unlearn?

Trenta?

(One's guess on age)

There was a time when little signs would come
And stroke the pleasing depths, from 'tween the walls
Of licked and fastened thought – when then would roam
The mischief of the mind 'yond hooded stalls
To distant lotus lands, and when the night
Was gawdy as the day when pictures grew
In size, in double size, in figments bright
With all the hues of what it never knew.
But now I am alone with many things
That have not worked and cannot work again,
Where every day a little ageing brings
And what will never be is ever pain.
And yet I touch a something in this dark,
And where naught moves much dangles on a mark.

29/10
(waiting for a letter)

Simplex

I have heard many words when sound was not,
And pondered long when song was gently heard;
I have revisited great lands forgot,
And smelt a person in a drifting word.
I have rewalked a yesterday today;
In having nought but thought upon the mind,
And I have, hidden Face, a little ray
Of Thine beheld when light was left behind.
For, Master, all is lost but this one last
And first of all that matters; I have none
But one, one only, one small friend too vast
To leave room for another – I have one:
I have Thee, Lord, I have Thee, have Thee all,
For I have grown to be but very small.

Loading the camera

What will you see, O eyes as dull as night,
Yet sharper than the sword in what you stab
Into the the annals of this printed light
That with one peep you for the morrow grab,
Lest Now be lost in Then without a trace
Of yesterday and yesterday once seen
And p'haps not twice rethought, were not its face
Observed, conserved, preserved where it had been?
When six and thirty twinkles of this eye
Have viewed th'unseen, what colours of what dawn
Will through these clouds have shone? O Master, why
Is little seen by hominids forlorn
Before 'tis seen and must be seen for aye,
For that no scrubbing can efface the day?

2/11
(All Souls)

I heard K – had been closed by the Holy See

A rumour is a loud amount of wind
And density of whisperings to scratch
The itching ear, yet, though we may rescind
The verdict of a lie, a little batch
Of truth oft lurks and works its mighty way
Through testimony's orbs, though false and far
From fact's domain – for though I smile and say
'Tis otherwise, I cannot wisdom bar.
For Truth without our aid knows well to stand
And wait till it be known, yet known it is
At times 'twixt Falsehood's teeth, and in my hand
I hold the Pow'r to make it be, not be,
For I can yet avoid this part of me.

Exit

The time had come, my friend, to say Goodbye,
And thou didst leave a word to show the way
In which thy bones to use... To die, to die
Was thy life's one demand, yet thou didst say
Not much of this thy brooding – thou didst not
Pause long o'er these long æons; thou didst think
To bid thy trouble be at last forgot,
And hope that Godhead would at this act wink.
Augustine! art thou gone? Art thou not here
To listen to my sin, as week on week
Thou patiently wouldst do? Was there not fear
Of losing more than life as thou didst seek
To end it all and send it all away
For ever and for ever in a day?

Λειτουργ ία

It is not well, it is not well, this haste
To hurry Thee and worry no more how
To spend upon a beauty and to waste
A moment on a glory, and to bow
At length in noseward wonder at it all –
Nay, nay, and to shape carefully a sound
And make an ectasy of granules small,
And with a stitch make earth to heaven bound –
For bodies have a soul, and as in flesh
I have felt many truths, so is there room
For language that can God and man enmesh
In regions just a little ’yond the gloom
Of workaday adorings made of void
Where once the masters with the angels toyed.

Irene

It would be peace to be at peace with thee
And these thy little siblings whom alone
Thy love calls into being – it would be
A paradise regained, one once long known
And cherished for its sound, for emptiness
Alone can fill the restless soul again,
And Thou, my Lord, didst my lost youth so bless
That I'll but hurt till I these years regain.
O! hiddenness of being all in one,
One only place, with but a Face unseen
For company, and melody alone
Made of the Silence that had ever been...
I would hear Thee again, my quiet Lord,
If Thou wouldst through this letter speak a word.

Montecassino

I have knelt here before beside this light
That has burnt on and on across the years
That join the day to day and night to night
But run their course beyond this realm of tears
In ways unknown, old friend, where thou art now
Upon a glory sitting – Benedict,
I have sighed here before, and thou didst show
In letters large the way that He had picked.
That was a childhood dream, and yet it was,
And now could be again, for this great pain
Of suff'ring known and missed a hurting has
That is too deep this time to lose again.
Good teacher, I will hurt until I know
That Love itself to loving has said, No.

4/11
(Cf. August 1972)

Canting

(first week as second cantor)

There are so many sounds that from the throat
Can come and find a home within the ear,
And though a melody is but a note
Within another weaved, I do not hear
But noise when these are struck, for something moves
Across the sky when there is beauty heard,
And in the little tingling that these grooves
And staves of thought direct there is a word
Not made of meaning but of flesh and sense
That strokes as it strikes softly on the soul
And fondles unmade matter - nay, skies dense
With little wings insensate sense the whole
Of what we here set forth, for in this place
There is the sound of oft a touching face.

7/11
(All Saints of Wales)

Writing

Upon a page there ages not a word,
There withers not a thought, there is but space
To linger 'neath the echo that was heard
And gaze upon the softly shining face
That faintly beams therein, and there is known
A yesterday whereon we placed our feet,
Our very weight, in inward phantoms shown
In curves and tidy strokes of pulsèd heat.
For there is part of us upon this line
That carries what we are, and we die not
As quickly as our flesh, for etchings fine
Can itch a long, long time for hours forgot.
And there is but a morrow here today,
For this hour left naught else ere't went its way.

Words

A word is but a little, little thing
That fills the universe with all it holds,
And in a tremored thought borne on the wing
Of wave and wave magnetic, air enfolds
A particle of soul, for there is more
Within a syllable of something meant
Than tappings of this drum – this little door
Through which these unwrit messages are sent:
There is a ray of glory in a sound
That will shine on, for where the glowing heart
Emits its pulsing gleams, hid forces pound
Upon the membranes of the inward part.
And we are not alone when with a word
That in pores not oft touched is softly heard.

Hurry

A haste is but a waste of running time,
And little was done well that was done ill
For that th'hour bid it happen: moments climb
Too quickly round th'uncaring face that still
Has care enough to tap a little more,
A little more again, a little less,
A little less again, less than before
We had than when we had this restlessness.
For there are moments that need time to be,
And we are fully made when made to stand
Upon a moving æon, that can see
Whence it has come into this ringing land
That has too many confines to be crossed
At walking pace, with just a moment lost.

Latin Mass

Day after day we mutter quietly
Alone and in a corner, with no eye
But Thine, eternal Vision, silently
Beholding this our magic, yet too nigh
Is Mystery to History's domain
To be too quickly pruned: there is a peace
In ling'ring in an age that did much gain
In losing all in wonder where words cease.
I have observed, my Lord, in serving Thee
Here where Thou art, unhurried and alone,
That there are many things that I can see
When looking well into the great unknown.
For there is here a something happening
That bids me to a fading æon cling.

Study

O Master, what are these, the heavy tomes
That look and look and ask, When wilt thou come
And spend a while with us? These little homes
Of softly sleeping truth, in which the hum
Of brains that laboured well may still be heard
Stand silently ere I pull back the door
That holds their privy musing, for a word
Is but a sleeping thought thought once before.
Yet there is of no fact a knowledge made,
A knowing never learned, a growing wise
That eyes did not absorb, for though I paid
In fortunes vast for these, at times two eyes
All sealed but to the dark have seen more sound
Than many, many words have ever found.

In the cellar

(with the Sisters)

The visage oft beheld and held to be
A something of great weight moves not unseen
Across the stage whereon the phantasy
Of being all bids man his being preen
With glories, each by long trisagion
By lesser glories sung – nay, many bask
In bliss of limelight that can but look on
And on and on at such a marvel mask.
Yet there move hither, thither some untrained
At acting but a part, a little part,
And spend a childhood and a maidhood strained
At but one perfect thing, and shine apart,
Far, far apart from e'en a passing eye
That might perhaps have giv'n a passing sigh.

Write a poem on me

(Sr. Arpana)

And yet, my wimpled sister, thou dost want
A little patting and a stroking pen,
And with a hidden fondle gently hunt
For touches never known, for little men
Can touch e'en still the maid within, within,
That never went away; nay, there are some
Who know not what they are, and are not in
The habit that they carry as their home.
My sister, my sweet sister, walk awhile
In this thy sweet unknowing – thou art well
To ask but for a mark to trace a smile
That this world will not see, but when the knell
Rings in its turn for thee, wilt hear it said,
"A little angel once for roses bled."?

Nun

What is a nun, if not a little world
That One alone may tread, and that no soul
May share? What bear the letters of a word
So short that they long mesmerize the whole
Of growing womanhood? What works within
The tingling impulse to be felt no more
A part of earthly being? What steps in
To this abyss of wanting to ignore?
O myst'ry veiled, I see but part of you,
Yet know a little more than you may feel,
For there is something strange that siblings new
Have like the ancients touched as they did kneel
Not far from where we are, not very far,
And we are many myriads where we are.

Hermit

O Master, to be free from heavy things
That are not made of Thee – to be, to be
Alone where all the sound of Being sings
But lightly in the air: to be with Thee,
And with none other ever – Thee alone,
And at Thy Face to gaze amazèdly
Until the burning wonder is outblown
By sleep that dreams Thee all eternally:
To have Thee and to hold Thee, Master, all,
All, all alone in holding, to win One
And lose the cumbered many, to hear call
My name by none, none other 'neath the sun –
Oh! Love! I would this have, and have no more,
For I have held Thee closely once before.

Mount Tabor

I will go back, I will go back to this
Across the sea,
For there is hurt within a wanted bliss,
And I'm yet free
To vow a higher and a higher word
Than one not well
By Thee, my Witness, heard.
A better may be done within a vow,
And there can be
Another half lived well, now, even now –
Eternity
Recalls and calmly calls from years once seen:
Come, walk again
Where only youth has been.
I will come home, and be a little while
Upon a shore
That I have often trod, and hear a smile
Beam as before,
E'en through the heavy clouds that severed day
From day once known
To hold an ancient ray.
For there is joy not in a pulsing heat,
But one soft felt
Again, again where once we placed our feet
And gently knelt,
Not where there is much mirth, but where there is
Enough, enough
Alone of what is His.
O Solitude! I will breathe in again,
I will be near
The Nearness that is nearest unto pain
That has no fear
To be a waste of being, but to be,
To be, be well
In ending utterly.

Trust

There was a night when I lay down my head
Upon a lap, and slept while wide awake
On this unmade yet softly padded bed
That man with all his craft did never make –
An evening, 'twas, when nothing much was heard
Except a little tap that came and went
And came again more strongly, till a word
Broke silence and asked gently what it meant.
'Twas told in scarce a whisper that 'twas prayer,
But prayer, that did move then, but prayer so deep
That it moved all that was not moving there,
For in the stillness I heard one heart leap.
And I thought how 'twas good to be at peace
With God and Woman when all flesh did cease.

From our own correspondent

A lover thou wast not, my little friend,
But only one that knew and understood
What 'twas without a word sharp words to mend
And what to touch with neither flesh nor blood.
Thou wast not one to push or crush the soul
With hymenæan magic, thou wast not
A one to stroke the part to move the whole
Or alter by a tugging word my lot.
Yet others have gone by, and done strange deeds
That were not meant for us, and eyes have gone
To other senses, fed on other needs,
And in their doings have long hours undone.
But thou didst want not much, and such alone
May without owning one one ever own.

Unberührt

(Sr. Subhashini)

What is this part of Woman that knows all,
And more than all? Of what is made this sense
That catches moving particles so small
That not e'en air can bear? What morsels dense
With emanating Man make thus to stir
The dormant still capillaries unseen
Untouched, unknown, untravelled where there were
No pulses sent, where none had ever been?
O virginhood, I stood so close with you
To something very huge in little maids
That were not meant to know, yet meanings knew
From sources I knew not, and knowledge fades
When introduced to knowing, that no man
Or angel trained in heav'n e'er capture can.

Quomodo cantabimus?

To sing is to be borne upon the wings
Of happiness and sorrow twice sustained,
And there is in the melody that sings
Of broken man the calming of the pained
And severed parts – there is a gath'ring sigh
Of sorrow that tomorrow can return
With but a hint of healing, when the cry
Can into musèd lulling slowly turn.
For in the air when there is something heard
That has come from afar, there are not notes
Made but of vibrant cords: there is conferred
Upon naught else but these our little throats
A mystery that history knew well,
For there is in a song all Heav'n, all Hell.

13/11
(All Saints of the Order)

Birthday

To be a little older than before
When we stood on this point; to want to be
Where we had been; to be, yet be no more
The fulness in the half that was once free
To waste a little time ere it moved on
Unhurried and unworried as the day
That has in coming many days undone
And hidden many secret hours away –
O! moments, come and gone, to be with you
Upon a point our own, to feel, to tell
The hurt of but an instant passing through,
And in a chime to hear a distant knell:
This is to hurt where hurting is not seen,
For to be here is to be having been.

Ἡσυχία

O Joy! I will return! I will return
To Paradise regained! The very walls
That stood and bid the blood all life unlearn
Stand yet, and still the sound of Life recalls
The hermit to his home. O! roaming Grace,
I will not let thee go, I will not leave
This touch unfelt, I will here touch this Face
Again, again: this time I'll to Love cleave.
For, Master, I have let Thee pass before,
And lost Thy gentle fondling, and have found
That there is but one moment on this shore
That will cross Lethe's stream, and one sole sound
That will be heard again in that long dream,
And 'tis the gentle music of a gleam.

Beatified

A failing is a worm in sanctity,
And Compromise a wriggled yield that gives
A yield to every other: clarity
Is dimmed, and dimmed again, when one soul lives
A-halting 'tween two pulls, and there is more
In one consent that bent the heavy will
Than bending of one precept, for before
The fall of all there is much falling ill.
O stars now lit, tread on these clouds, whose sound,
Made but of growing music and high song,
An echo in my heart this morn hath found
Of something heard before, where I did long
With you to walk this way, this lonely way,
To anthems that began upon a day.

2/11
(after ceremony)

Homeward bound

I shall not walk again upon this road,
Nor shall I linger ’twixt eternity
And moments rattling by, for where we strode,
While waiting for the morrow yet to be,
Our feet we place not twice: we here move on,
And on, my brother, on, for we have seen
No pocket in the wind that will have gone
Tomorrow where Tomorrow will have been.
This is the hour on which I softly tread,
But I now hold the morrow in my hand,
And I have pow’r o’er hours as yet unsaid,
Whose sound will stand for e’er if I here stand.
There is a will that can the course of all
In one charged second change beyond recall.

20/11
(resolving)

Altar of Luther's last Mass

Art thou at peace, good priest; art thou at peace
Where mighty voices move no more the earth,
Where double vision and long probings cease
And knowing is the all of pain or mirth?
Couldst thou here come again and walk this way
And tread upon this step that was the last
To hold thee close to Godhead for a day
Ere thou another take that would It blast,
Wouldst thou a little moment ponder on
Before receding from this holy height
Where early hours perhaps in bliss had gone
In loving gaze upon this hidden light,
That thou unveiled dost see, I hope – I hope,
For do eyes all well see that so well grope?

Altar of St. Maximilian Kolbe's first Mass

The grace of having and of having well
What has been wanted long – the grace of all
Who come this way and at the sacred bell
Hold high the One who to this height can call
The heart that could want else, the grace of Pow'r
Unfelt but known, and owned for e'er and e'er:
This was the little movement of this hour
Thine own, for thou didst hold not angels there
But Him that held them too, and bid them come
And gaze upon amazing hidden grace
That, coming still, bids me too hence come home
And for a time do naught but love this Face
That thou canst see, my friend – that thou canst see,
See well enough to bid Him call e'en me.

Sister

There is within a woman's breast a world
We have not seen or known, but only felt,
And in the many movements that men hurled
Into the great Machine, the soul that knelt
And did but love awhile, moved all the earth
A little further onward to its home
While some worked well, too well, with little mirth
To calm the counted moments ere they come.
O! goodness hidden yet, where none may walk
Or enter in and please – for Pleasure here
Is none, unless it be of distant talk
That touched not much beyond the chastened ear –
Is this the all of loving, or can we
Beyond the veil an unmade mother see?

Risk

This is the time when many times have been,
The day that brings another from afar.
This is the hour that magic hours has seen,
And yesterdays beholds there where they are
Upon the mem'ry's screen – this is the day
Wherein a hood was giv'n, wherein a name
Changed e'en the soul that wore it – changed it, nay:
Remade it what it was, the same, the same!
For there is no unmaking of a soul,
Or e'er a call recalled – there is no more
A half of us when we the very whole
Have set upon an altar once before.
A monk I am, a monk I'll be again,
And I'll throw all, but one lost peace to gain.

10/11
(St. John Roberts)

Murder?

("One of the prostitutes was murdered last night, near the house.")

When there is darkness man moves not alone,
But 'neath the moon a hand unseen draws on
To acts of deeper black, wherein the groan
Of unpreparèd pain is quickly gone
Into the great unknown, where none shall see
Or hear or touch again what stirs no more
The hungered body and the gilded plea
For favours where shared favours went before.
O! sadness doubly deep! To peep at these,
Our flesh and blood, that open where no love
Can enter in or with a touch appease
The gaping of the all that man can move,
This is to sigh that some can give too much,
For more can travel 'neath a gentler touch.

Dream

To dream is not to be, yet 'tis to be
What deeper being is: we are alone
With what we are when we our inwards see
And follow for a while a path unknown
That we know well, for 'tis what we most are,
And we through knowing this, believing this,
Can meet again a stranger from afar –
What we once were – and feel an ancient bliss:
This, this is what I was and what I am,
This spectred habit worn and borne again,
For though an unwise blessing did years damn
To wand'ring long, I did this night regain
A happiness too deep to be let fall,
And 'twas a dream that, lying, truth did call.

First sermon

A word is but a pulse of thinking heard
And gathered where it rests, where others lie
In somnolence untroubled, for the word
Unuttered e'er again can calmly die
Within th'entombèd regions that the brain
Hides e'en from its own gaze – for we are not
All ears, nor can the mind hear all again
That through the air did pass ere 'twas forgot.
And yet a dying sound can linger on,
And there is pow'r within a little noise,
For, though we travel on when words have gone
The way of every sound, there can yet poise
Betimes before our eyes a drifting thought
In th'engine of Forgetting somehow caught.

Betrayed

I did love well, I did love very well –
Too well not to feel this: there are some pains
That none will ever know, for e'en in Hell
There is a demon for th'elysian plains
That ne'ermore will be seen, and he beholds
The essence that hurts on and thinly on,
While here the soul unseen in hiding holds
The agony of what elsewhere was done.
O! Womankind, there is a goodness deep
That in its op'ning wide to other parts
Can weaker goodness foul. Were I to peep
Through th'eyelids of the Night, what unlearned arts
Would I so throughly master? What are these
Red cloths that e'en th'Altar never sees?

Bouquet amid condoms

A flow'r for but a little soul that went
Without a flurry to the hidden land
Whence all have come with numbered moments lent
By Hands unseen – O! last, O! longest stand
Into the night wherein a heavy work
Is done beneath the moon... Too soon the end
Of this great task unfinished did here lurk,
And this last act of wanting fast unbend.
O! little while that held a long, long age,
Short moment that the æons opened wide –
What chapters of what faults lie on this page
Now closed for ever where long mem'ries hide?
What, little child, lies now where thou dost lie
Alone, alone, beneath a lonely sky?

(It seems that the 32 year old Colombian actually died of a heart attack, possibly drug-related. There was a bouquet this morning where her body had been.)

Posso chiederti un favore?

A button that is pushed and pushed again,
And yet again, again, where moments bid
All halt upon this line – a little pain
That blasts the tranquil ear, where thoughts are hid
'Neath pillows and 'neath tomes and papers dense
With meaning and with gleaning of much weight
That must needs enter in: a pulling thence
Of all in gentle pressure never late –
This is my thumb's small duty, this is all
I have to think to do, yet think I must,
For though a little thing be this my call,
It is enough that all one man entrust
With duty that moves all, for one to be
Fidèle, fidèle, unchanged Fidelity.

Drug

(dopo il caffè)

The body and the mind can do great things
Alone, and greater still when gently pushed
By molecules of sense whose essence clings
To needs unroused, caroused till all is hushed
Save this new need and craving – we are not
Aware of what we are, nor are we near
The zenith of our being when our lot
Remains well bound by long ancestral fear.
Yet there is in this bondage liberty
From bonds too great to hold, and though I be
A timid morsel of eternity,
I home will safely go, for I can see
That granules in a liquid move enough
Of th'untrained soul, without a jerk more rough.

Auferte ista hinc

Amid the hours that move and move us on,
Amid the spaces wherein moments rest,
Amid the workings done and never done
And pausèd waitings by a hollow blest,
There can be times when time need not be moved
As quickly as it is, there can be days
Too filled with force of filling – nor improved
Are happenings by happening always:
There is a place, there is a holy place
Where nothing need much move, where quietly
The beams that hover near can have a space
To be perceived, received just quietly.
For we need not do much, but do much well,
And oft a softer doing more can tell.

Omega

(ceasing to wear a watch)

When I think on, and wonder what may be
Tomorrow and tomorrow after this,
When many bells have rung and silently
I sink into the grave and quiet bliss
Or torment that will last, I ponder on
Upon this mystic duty of an hour
That must ere it burn out be wholly done,
And gaze upon this instrument's tapped pow'r.
O little gadget, tip into the void
The sweat of all that beat thee, clap the skies
Till they too lessons heed, and be annoyed,
My angry friend, that I am not yet wise,
Yet I will take a moment to be free,
For time is not in punctuality.

Superiority?

It is all one, it is all one, the whole
Of being here on earth. There is no saw
That found a sharpened way 'tween flesh and soul
Or two of us that moved, for this our core
Is all of what we are, and we can do
No more than be well made, though fade we shall
In one of these our brethren, though it too
May seek a little while a pedestal.
There is, my Love, no wonder for a man,
Nor for a part of man, nor for a life
Made of a man's own part, for though we can
Make ripples for a time, there is no strife
That Act or Contemplation made to be
Of use, were't not Osmosis used by Thee.

Julian

O child of bygone pain, O little noise
Once heard without a word upon the page
That holds thee still, where stilled in gentle poise
Are thoughts that flutter yet 'tween age and age –
O happy child! O child all wild with God
That brought thee home, nay, kept thee homeward bound
Within a home all His, thy feet have trod
A land that I have known and homely found.
O sister, elder sister, where thou art
Hard by the Ear of all, recall that here
The morsels of a doubly broken heart
Would find a place to love, a place as near
To this world's end as did thy loving hide,
For none that knew this once can else abide.

Si è spento il sorriso

What is a smile? What is a beam of light
Within a shining visage? What is this
That twinkles 'twixt two lids not fastened quite,
And scatters yet a modicum of bliss
Upon a damnèd heart? What muscles move
Within a soul so fine that shine it must
Until it warm another and remove
A fear of eyeing what no man may trust?
O wonder of a look that can books hold,
With neither word nor whisper! – Little change,
Made of a sparkle new so very old
That Eve's first child it knew! – Thou dost arrange
A meeting 'tween two worlds upon a gleam,
And some said more on earth than it would seem.

A gleam: Dad's picture – at La Trappe.

Bell

I hear a sound upon a distant land
Far, far away,
Made of the same, this same, that this my hand
Forms here this day,
But not of wire and worry made to be
The Master's voice
From pressed Eternity.

Nay, nay, I hear a sound, and hear it well
Across the sea,
And I behold the frame of this one bell
That will be free
To call when He will call, to call upon
The depth of night
That need not slumber on.

I hear a voice of calling in the air,
That will not die,
And in a sorrow there is something there
That moves on high,
For there I hear again an ancient joy
That filled the night
With love no morn could cloy.

I hear the matin cry within the stars
That vigil keep,
And in the firmament no hurry mars
The eyes that peep
In cherub gaze upon a world apart
Where soon again
A sound shall hold my heart.

(On *Lead, kindly light*)

Amidst angels

(at the altar)

There is a gleam of joy the heart knows not
How well to feel, not made of reeling sense
Or of a tingled pleasure, where moods hot
With warming much such moments carry hence
As come not back unless in need twice grown,
But of a Godhead's flesh, for I have touched
The tremor of long age; I have been shown
The Cause in which the centuríes are clutched.
It shall be well, it shall be very well,
All manner of a thing – nay, there is nought,
Unless it be the pedigree of Hell,
That is not, has not been, will not be wrought
By this, Thy loving gaze, O Ecstasy,
That hast thought long on how best all to see.

Quid hic agis, Elia?

To sit and listen and to wait awhile
For something more to be – to be alone
With nothing but a thought, and to beguile
The urgencies that these our moments own –
To be no more than nothing in a space
Not filled with any thing, to be but here
And to be here, all here, all in a place
Made all of nothing else, and there to hear –
To hear, that is, the sound of listening:
'Tis to hear one small thing, for when no more
We pulse, and hard repulse all hastening
And linger for a while where once before
We heard hours pass, this is to pass along
A chasm where no travell'r lingers long.

Heri, hodie et in sæcula

(Oui d'un[e] ermite)

Je me reçois, mon Dieu, je me reçois
De Toi, le tout du tout, car aujourd'hui
Un néant, tout un néant, Te perçoit
Au fond de ce qui vient, car même lui
Qui vit sans Te revoir au Paradis
Vit ici de Ta vie, et il peut faire
Un rien de ce bien, car Tu dis
Son nom dans un Jamais qu'il ne peut taire.
Ô Vie! Haleine, Toi qui me respires,
Toi seul que je dois voir, Toi seul qui es,
Fais qu'en la nuit où Tu enfin retires
Ce souffle de mon jour, qu'il sera fait,
Ce rêve d'une nuit, ce bruit d'un Dieu,
Ce Oui d'éternité fait en ce lieu.

Hæc est via: ambula in ea

This is the day, this is the blessèd night
When all on earth did cease, when joy and pain
In undressed form came in and entered quite
The length of seven long years – I hear again
The distant matin call that in the rest
Of that first night I heard: I taste, I smell
The studied essences that there were blest
By hallowed hours still rocked by that same bell.
I cannot be away from this my home,
And if it will not be, then I shall find
A way to make the years again here come
Ere I for e'er leave moving years behind.
The will of man is but a little thing,
But there are times when days to one day cling.

Asillo

What is a worry but a laboured thought,
A moment doubly lost, a tragedy
Twice lived, a burden borne and brought
To hours it did not own, a comedy
Viewed by eternal Vision, that had ways
And time enough to think long upon this
And see its causèd end with placid gaze,
Untroubled by a ripple amid bliss?
O Problem, grow and grow and fill the world
With none but thee alone, and have thy way
Tomorrow, but today this hour has hurled
Thy face from this my staring, for today
Will never be tomorrow, and thy snare –
Is it not this, to place each morrow there?

Letter in the Bible

Rest now, good friend, rest on; the time is gone:
No more shall scribblings travel on a page
From where this hand now lies, yet though 'tis done,
The work that they performed, there is not age
Or growing older in the Father's land
Where son meets son that was a son in turn
To Adam that all bore, and this kind hand
That penned a hurried word doth here return
Not from the tomb, but from the womb of hours –
The ancient calm where all things have an end,
And though where lies that face, the gentle pow'rs
Of loving come no more, this earth can lend
A particle or two to hold a sound
That I will hear again when home is found.

1995

This is the year wherein the world will be
Not what it was: this is the day that dawns
From morns afar, observed in ecstasy
Long gone, yet caught by some where Vision warns
Again upon this globe, this little ball
So heavy and so small, where all doth hang
'Twixt yesterdays and morrows that now call
A melody eternity once sang.
I have heard talk of thee, small virgin year
So huge that Time thee fears – I have been told
Such things as tingle in a piercèd ear
That trapped an echo of what hours unfold.
This is the day wherein the all is set,
And in one tick the æons this night met.

Hic habitabo, quoniam elegi eam

(Tabor)

O peace! O blessèd peace! This is the place
Where Heav'n to Earth is wed – this is the land
Wherein the universe has one small space
For me: this day a gentle Master's hand
A way through thickets huge has calmly brushed,
And from a distant world has homeward called
Where in a moment twenty years were hushed,
And in a look the flame of Youth recalled.
O land so vast and holy! Land of light
Wherein the world moves not, wherein the dark
Holds o'er the neon gloom a burning bright
Made of a vigil long, a song to mark
The pauses no more made – this, this alone
Is what I want upon this globe to own.

Stella Maris

(Convent, Dublin Bay)

Fe fydd ryw ddydd dawelwch yn y nen
Fel yn y dyfroedd hyn; fe ddaw yr awr
Y clywir eto lais y Wyry Wen
A wenodd gynt, wrth yngan gyda'r wawr
A dorrai dros y byd, y gair a roes
Ei chnawd i'r Gair ei Hun; fe fydd rhyw le
I ddianc eto'n ôl, fel gynt y ffois
Rhag sŵn yr hyn sydd fud i sain y Ne'.
Fe fydd, mi wn, rhyw gloch yn seinio cân
Y pethau hen fu ar yr ynys hon,
A chlywaf ddyfod eto nodau mân
Y siant ddi-lais, y côr fu echdoe'n llon.
Cans dof yn ôl o bell i bellter pur
Yr unig ing all leddfu gormod cur.

Four

This is the hour in which the night is rent;
By you, my sisters, on the em'rald shore;
The hour in which the air a voice once lent
To sound unmade, that had been made before
On Penmon's lapping waves; the hour alone
When flesh and flesh oft meet where no eye sees
The passage of a soul; the hour unknown
On earth, when heav'n – 'tis said – the chained soul frees:
This is the very hour when pow'rs move on
The globe to probe the pillows where we lie
Forgetting what we are, for much is done
When many slumber still 'neath th'unlit sky.
And I can not sleep well beneath a spell
That pulls upon a rope where dangles hell.

12/1
(Rome)

Μουσεῖον

A monk there was that had been once remiss
In praying and in saying all he should,
That had been left – 'twas thought – in depth of bliss
Whence – if these prints be true – he came and stood
Upon a cloud of fire and calmly left
A trace of burning bright, that might not be
All of a glory made, but one bereft
Of ever having been as thought had we.
A vigil there was kept where slept the bier
Of one but newly gone where all must go,
But 'twas one long, long passed that this scared seer
Here gazed upon and thought anon to know.
And know he did, and know shall we till none
Cares here to turn to see strange burning done.

15/1
(Purgatory Museum, near the Vatican)

Hell

There is a place beyond geography
Where pain is heard no more, where pain is all
That can be heard for evermore to be
The echo of the last unvoicèd call
No larynx made, where fade the very sounds
That matter for a while, for matter there
Is none, and where these lie 'yond Sleep's sweet bounds
There is a rest that is best taken ne'er.
O little field of stones, each silently
Awake upon strange rest, a story vast
Hangs on your chiselled words, and quietly
A pendulum rocks onwards at the last:
Amen. For aye. Amen. So shall it be.
Amen. For aye. Amen. It shall not be.

Rome

A year is but a notch in what is not,
For time is but a having been, and none
Has held a moment or beheld the little dot
That ended any hour or day here gone.
We sit upon a cloud and in the air
That separates two worlds we move along
To troubles unforeseen, and what seemed fair,
Viewed from afar, when known holds torments long.
'Twere better for a while to be untaught
Of morrows that were not, for pain enough
Is in a daylight's span, and joy unsought
Is oft a deeper than a bliss too rough.
And there is nothing in tomorrow's rays
As sure as but a tingle of today's.

30/1
(Anniversary of arrival)

Carthusian

There is no way to be what we are not,
And none to be again what yet we are.
O! pain! I cannot leave this land forgot
Or walk upon another! – E'en this star
That in the eve I'd watch from that warm cell
Upon a winter's night, calls from the sky
And bids a hidden tear of hiraeth well
From where a touch too tender came too nigh.
It is too much, the hurt of hurting ne'er
Again with pain well fondled; there is none
Or aught upon this globe to hold me there,
Thy work, sharp nib, that cracked that wall, now done.
Hid Light, shine darkly on. 'Neath altered name
I see in Erin's mist a home the same.

Exorcism

There is somewhere a pain beyond the world
Of sense, whence none returns to share a thought
Of ghostliness untold, yet in this word
Of eloquence demonic quite unsought,
But giv'n 'twixt grinding teeth, I see a sound
Of Raging incandescent where there is
No more a moment's cooling to be found,
Or company but fellowship all his...
"Together go..." – "Together none may be."
"Go thither whither God prepared a place..."
"No God made this: created it have we,
And for much loneliness there is much space."
And there are some that burn as I read on
And on and on on beamèd glories gone.

Fellowship

If thus it is to burn alone, alone
Upon a parted æon where no man
May share or know a little thought his own
For that another sent it – where none can
Hear aught but hurting noise, where poised are all
The pow'rs of severed soul 'tween what is not
And what can never be, then something small
'Gins to be hugely vast when 'twas forgot.
For I perceive that not to hold a soul
Asleep upon the breast, not to know well
The world therein that moves, or feel the whole
Of unfelt being in small sounds that tell,
Is to walk on upon a lonely road
Where damnèd spectres have no fixed abode.

Media

Means mediating meaning from afar
And moving many minds without a word
When moving on a leaf, or from a star
Suspended in the air where sounds are heard
By metal ears moved by strange wavicles
Of patterns sent to tremble something deep
In many breasts unseen – these particles
Of Naught at night a mighty vigil keep:
For gazing at a tabernacle new
Adorers watch and wait, and there is seen
Not chargèd ions coming into view
But all of man and more upon a screen
That holds a mesmered eye with other eyes
Agog upon a current in the skies.

Wavicles: coinage of physics master at school, to explain nature of electro-magnetic forces, that act with properties both of waves and of particles.

Den Worten aufmerksam lauschte

I have heard oft a sound and heard it not,
Looked at a gaze and tapped not what was said;
I have seen in an eye a thought forgot
Too soon, for 'twas too quickly hither shed.
I have heard many things that shall remain
Unheard again, for I was unaware
Of all that moved therein, and mutt'rings plain
Will pass to whence they came, for none was there:
None there, I say, none was at home to be
A host to but a presence – none stood still
To hold or catch a being, or to see
What warmed and waited 'fore a guarded chill.
I have not listened well, but heard too much
Stray sound that found no ear where too might touch.

Dawn over Rome

The Sabbath rest is best heard when no sound
Removes hypnotic dreams, and gleams of light
Break softly without haste, and dawn is found
Without the aid of jolting – when the night
Has time to be, and time to be unknown,
Or just a little known, known just enough
To be caressed in thinking, when alone
The virgin body calms a phantom's bluff.
The noise of many movements in the dark,
The shuffling of a world, the sleep not ta'en
By souls too long awake, the restless spark
Of life that will not die... – I hear the pain
Of many hearts that sleep not well, I hear
The ghost of travelled Babel yawning here.

Hagios hagios hagios

O Light, I see Thee not, but feel Thy face:
There is a presence here; there is, my Lord,
Not matter in this little, little space
Made of the ground of being, but of Word
That bid all being be – I see, I see
Enough, my hidden Love, to love Thee well;
I understand that standing here will be
The last command of Heaven and of Hell.
My Lord, I shall not go again afar,
I shall not gaze into another eye:
The better part is here, for where we are
There is a music 'twixt the earth and sky.
And Will and Will can meet in but a look
Of gazing Godhead that a sharp aim took.

Rereading

The missive that I hold within my hand
Comes not from woman kind but Godhead's ink
That 'mid a crumbled life yet here doth stand
And bid me read again and calmly think
Of Majesty untaught, unvowed to live
The dying of the death where energy
Is none, where done is all I have to give,
Where all the pow'r of hours is lethargy.
O! spark in this long dark, O! little thought
That hast been brave enough to brave the great
Of high authority, with utter nought,
I'll come, I'll come with nothing but this weight
Of heavy, heavy trust – I'll come, sweet soul,
And in this desert isle the æons stroll.

Last words in solitude

Seigneur, je quitte cet oratoire, où je t'ai trouvé, où j'ai passé tant de temps avec toi. Toi seul, tu sais ce que l'avenir contient. Mène, douce Lumière, là où tu voudras. Je m'abandonne à toi, car tu m'aimes, car tu sais, mieux que moi, ce que tu fais. Adieu, cellule! Adieu, oratoire! Adieu, lieu de souvenirs qui ne s'effaceront jamais. O Solitude! toi seul connais les cœurs de ceux qui t'habitent.

(4.45h., Sélignac, 15:2:84)

I see again the words once quickly writ
Upon an hour wherein the hours were rent,
Wherein the pain of parting did here split
The soul that was for strolling never meant
And what had held it safe – I see again
The happiness of youth where truth was found
And lost in one confounding, in one gain
Of freedom unto every mercy bound.
I see upon this page a moment long
That ten years, nay, and more, hath waited here,
And, though I sit alone, a gentle throng
Of mem'ries whispers softly in my ear,
Return, we are yet here, for yesterday
Knew well that thou'dst but walk a little way.

Peace

(after coming across St. Bruno – and vowing)

An accident was never upon earth,
Or on the globe a meeting, or a chance
Event that went not far in this its birth
Beyond the realm of little things we glance
To see as here we wonder how we came
So suddenly again to yesterday –
O! Yesterday! Today thy gentle name
Bears all my marred tomorrows hence away:
I will return to this thy tranquil light,
And 'neath one tender face that shone before
I will walk back to where a threshold bright
Once beamed enough to woo me to this door.
I will here knock again, and will not go
Away again from what I know, I know...

17/2
(S. Maria degli Angeli)

Subiaco

O Saint of God, that trod a lonely way
Into the dark unknowing, where no man
Could follow, nay, or come and some word say
To still the sound of silence, that here can
Beat loudly on the heart that is alone
With naught but absent loving, only heard
By part of what we are – here, here was known
The gentle echo of a pulsing word:
A word, good friend, was given and was shed
Upon a page to be – a page of thought
At whose soft beck the centuries would tread
And turn and turn upon a bidding caught
'Tween Heav'n and Earth in but a *speco* deep
Where three hid years did dark battalions keep...

Rite

O world apart! The art of being hid
Within a cloud so bright that light alone
Is seen by th'inward eye – this 'tis that bid
The three that climbed that ridge and heard th'unknown
Not say or utter aught of what no man
Had hitherto been shown: this was the word
That bade all words not be, for list'ning can
Be but in holding well a tremble heard.
O! Tabor, here I climb again that place
That on thy feast I walked – here, here again
The incense sweet that drugged a magic space
Hath dazed the mem'ry's cells with quiet pain
Of wanting much, of wanting such a God
As none did long forgo that hither trod.

Rite: Maronite Liturgy.
O! Tabor: Recalling Sunday morning at Meteora, 6th Aug. 1972

C'è la Presenza!

(Holy Father's words at Siena)

Will this yet happen, Master hid and veiled
'Neath matter's strangest form – 'neath matter made
To be deformed, unmade, yet unassailed
By Time's eroding vice here where must fade
E'en Youth's once freshest bloom in other flesh
'Neath form of bread, where Godhead laid His Head
And slept upon an æon, while His mesh
Of causes ever caused He windward sped:
Will this still happen yet, my hidden Lord,
Once seen upon the Mount – wilt Thou yet come
Into my little hands, and will the word
Tap Godhead's marching softly, softly home
To rest upon an altar we can make
Upon a long long pause for wasting's sake?

Time's eroding vice: a reference to the ongoing eucharistic miracle of the incorrupt Hosts preserved in Siena, whither, because of a seminar, I had been unable to return (having been there once in 1975) with some of the brethren.

Sero te amavi

To know that we are wanted, wanted well,
That there is here a Hand, and that an Eye
Doth placidly gaze on while noisome Hell
Breaks loose upon a speck – nay, that the sky
Lies tranquil o'er the world while heard is all
Th'unpleasantness of Man: this is to know,
My God, that Thou hast yet a time to call
To moments of hid fondling 'neath this glow.
O Tent of Meeting, I have heard herein
The sound of silent trembling, where a wing
Oft fluttered o'er a Guest who deep within
A smoke of Presence dense did but one thing:
O Love! I heard Thee loving, I have heard
The sound that found no home within a word.

Grace

The will of man is but a particle
Of unmade matter dense whence ever flows
The morrow that it shapes: no miracle
Could be where this was not, and where this blows
The whim of days will follow, for no man
Tomorrow stands where Yesterday was not,
And there are hours betimes when moments can
In tapping on a will still trap our lot.
O! Vision of a Cosmos, Providence
That moved a moment hither many times
In hope of but a catching, turn not hence
Again in vain, for here a something rhymes
With patterns seen before upon this shore
Of nearness oft so near and now no more.

Sélignac

When I recall how Monday used to come
To smile upon a cell, when sun and moon
Would calculate their movements that the dumb
Might speak again a little, and when noon
Would bring a hidden shiver lest a cloud
Obscure or even halt a blest reprieve,
Then something in the breast a sigh too loud
For other ears to hear doth softly heave.
My brethren, of what nothings of a bliss
Do you make sadness sweeter as I write?
My friends, do you think I think not of this
That was my soul, our soul, our common light?
And thou, of all friends kindest, closest, where
Are those blue rays that meant that home was there?

5.30 a.m.

A virgin is unused, and this the night
That mingles with the morn is born of hope,
And yet I hear a word that one did write
As he with eventide of life did grope:
I have done many things – my day I used
In pouring on the many... And he went
Into the rest of night that day refused,
Aware of this alone, that 'twas o'erspent.
There is much hurry in the harried soul,
And many nerves twitch hard as through each pore
Of being quickly roused is oozed the whole
Of what we deeply are, for once before
I knew too what it was to stroke the eyes
Of dawn with just enough of Paradise.

Le bon Dieu nous le renvoie

(Novice master's words, 1984)

O memories of loving! Memories
Affixed to atoms huge of captive light
That particles of magic slowly freeze
Upon a day that dies not with the night –
O! parts of yesterday that came this way
Not once but once too oft in blitzed attack,
How can I stand unshielded from this ray
Of essence that doth naught but presence lack?
O! stones that held my soul, in stillness stand
Upon this page that ages not as they
That on it smile, for while this little hand
Makes noise upon this line, it knows a way
Once used to hold a word, a word unheard
But felt where knelt the hearts that hid the word.

5/3
(after seeing pictures of La Trappe)

La cellule N vous attend

(Dom Siméon's letter, 1976)

O Sister, gentle Mother, little thing
Of loving never known, whence came this gift
Of Joy in which the earth no mirth to sing
Enough could find, or music sound to lift
Into the skies to praise the Hand that planned
A place of peace where cease the voices dark
That haunt e'en on the page? – O! little hand
That penned a sound so sweet, I kiss thy mark:
For there is on this globe a place for us
Prepared from long, long days – the tears of yore
Are dried upon a ray of meaning thus
Sent through the air where sharp marks went before.
O! mystery of history upturned,
This night a mighty pleasantness hath burned.

5/3
(Reading Sr. Irene's message)

Research

O Master Adam, I can feel thy soul
And touch the pulse that penned this little page
Whereon thou speakest still, for e'en the whole
Of long oblivion's yawn and heavy age
Can dampen not the tremor in this line
Of teeming ink that links in lying here
My mind to thine that made it, for, though thine,
It is mine own that makes it now come near.
O! myst'ry of the quill, that still dost move
'Tween heart and buried heart, what is a thought
Held once by thee and placed within a groove
That can guide all my hours or lie as nought
'Twixt dust and rust that never heard a sound
Or spared a thought for someone never found?

Mulier fortis

(Hermit's letter)

O sadness deep! O sadness doubly deep!
To know that years have come and years have gone
Into th'abyss of Happ'nings that shall keep
Their vigil long on Mem'ry's tale to run
For ever, ever more – to know that we
Missed in one hour what did have pow'r to move
All living's breath aright: to know and see
The day that marred it all – this is to prove
A hurt that hurts too much, for such is not
Within man's pow'r to heal, and yesterday
Must ever be tomorrow unforgot
By him that once chose that 'twould walk this way.
O sister of a peace, had I done this
But yesterday, would one day have held bliss?

Oxford

I think upon a moment that was not,
A joy that was not had, a day but shared
With friends that had it well, when this fair lot
Had been too quickly spurned by one ensnared
By grace too strong that could not long await –
Or so it seemed – the morrow's calmer day:
I think again upon the heavy weight
That in an unweighed No for ever lay.
O! hurt of but a wanting! What are we
That want too much and such in wanting lose
As shall be wanted aye – what can this be,
The folly of an hour with pow'r to choose:
To choose the placid days of ordered age
That p'haps would have traced naught on this sad page?

Amma

(...if you were to come...)

O bliss! O utterness of bliss! To know
We can with loving be, all, all alone
To hear the sound of nothings that can glow
Upon a tranquil dark, and there to own
The Godhead in a touch that sparked the night
Of cosmic dust thrust into ordered range
By Wisdom's 'waited word – to stroke the Might
Of Fatherhood and feel a Warming strange:
This, this is to be ne'er regretting more
The folly of a throw – this is to bow
To forces o'er our heads that moved before
Upon this globe where probed lost stars that now
Walk on upon a glory looking down
To see if we'll brave Deity full shown.

Elisabeth

(de la Trinité)

O eyes! O eyes! I have seen these before
In moments sweet when eye and Eye did meet.
O little eyes so huge through which did pour
The gazing of a soul, what gentle heat
Of Womanhood did in a pupil lurk
And pierce a tent of Dwelling – what are these
Now seeing where no sight this night can work
On quenchèd cells wherein no membrane sees?
O mem'ries of a looking! I can see
Again a cell – another – where these shone
Within a week of looking long at Thee,
My Love, our Love, for looking with a nun
Unseen, I 'gan to see what of a gaze
Was calling unto looking not two ways.

9/3
(as Dom Siméon is dying in Sélignac)

Yn d'oleuni y gwelwn oleuni

(Bedd-argraff Dad)

Cei orffwys bellach, gyfaill, yn yr hedd
Na ddaw'r un waedd i'w ddiffodd – cei yn awr
Ymgolli yn y wawl o gylch y Wedd
A'th alwodd adre'n ôl, a thon hud sawr
Y thus lle plŷg y corau yn eu cân
Cei ddysgu'r siant sydd hen, ac yn y Wên
A roddodd wawr i'r sêr cei weld yn fân
Bob echdoe a fu'n llenwi'r llyfrau hen.
Cwsg yn dy flaen, fwyn ffrind, cans mynd a wnawn
Yfory ac yfory tua'r hwyr
Sydd gynnar iawn iti ers y prynhawn
A ddaeth, a aeth, gan newid oll yn llwyr.
Cans daw y dydd a'th gofia, ac wrth ddod
Daw cof y llewych gymerth ran o'm bod.

Pervigilans

Qu'es-tu, Quies? Qu'es-tu, secret de Dieu
Connu de ceux qui fuient vers ce saint mont
D'où tout se voit? O! paradis, O! lieu
Tracé sur nulle carte! – Ici les sons
Ne sont plus si sonores, car les voix
Trop fortes portent mal la vérité,
Et seul en ce Horeb je vois, perçois
Le temps qui prend le ton d'éternité.
O! moment pur, où jeûne l'âme enfin
Vêtue du grand Silence! Sabbat long! –
Des âges qui ont eu en leur déclin
Le temps de visiter cet horizon
Où nul ne passe sans enfin se taire –
Tais-moi, car seul le Rien est à faire.

O post me! O per me! O ad me!

(Words of Adam Scot)

O Christ, alive and well – O Christ of fire
Here standing in the sun, O Son of Man,
Of essence God of God, to Godhead higher
Rise into clouds that hide Thee 'mid light wan
From looking at Thy shining – gaze upon
The ball that Thou didst tread and shalt recall
To order at the Ordering whereon
The all shall be what can alone be all:
Thy toy, O King, that with a finger's pow'r
Thou didst bid be and happily combine
In cause and cause entwined at perfect hour
In calcule of Time's dawn born once to shine –
O Lamb once slain, now standing, stand in might
Upon a cosmos dreamt upon a night.

See! I do all things

(Norwich, Mt Tabor)

Is this the morn I leaned upon a stone
That hid a friend unseen, who had been ours
In our own hallowed land – a friend well-known
Like this the blest fair scribe of these walled hours
Whose heavy words I hold – , is this the day
I prayed with groans unheard to be heard well
Where this last ghost of glory shewed the way
To th'anchorhold's soft holding of all hell?
O heav'n of hurting bliss, what thing is this
That will not let me go? I cannot be
Alone with any other, for 'tis His
The eye of Foresight far, 'tis His I see
Upon a letter and a letter sweet
Where many endings of long wending meet.

14/3
(recalling Dom Damien's tomb, Camaldoli, 1985)

Texts

(Rereading the pages of Butler's Lives that converted me to Catholicism)

These are the sounds resounding from afar
Upon the patient page that quietly
Holds Yesterday's sweet voice: these letters are
The wires, the same, through which once silently
A mighty message came – these are the prints
Wherein Truth placed His feet and left a word,
Not of a loudness bellowed but shed hints
All of a tingle gathered where thoughts stirred.
O! thought all nought, yet of all wrought the source,
I hear again thy coming: humming close
To mine own kernel's knowing, this soft force
Was all that bade me shift – this little dose
Of light upon a night showed me my home
Hard by an ancient cloud where youngsters roam.

O tyn
Y gorchudd yn y mynydd hwn

Nid oes na hedd na gorffwys dan y fron
A wybu Heddwch gynt lle nad oedd dyn
Na sŵn y byd yn cyffwrdd mwy â hon
Y galon gnawd y ddoe fu'n curo'n un
Â thangnef nef y Nef – ni all fod mwy
Nag Un yn gymar i guriadau cudd
Y deunydd brau a ddeil yn un y ddwy
Fan elfen Bod yfory ddaw yn rhydd.
O Feistr y gorwelion, gwêl yn awr
Un na all droi yn ôl at ddydd a fu
Yn adlais gormod lleisiau, cans rhy fawr
Yw'r hiraeth yn y golled yma sy.
Ni allaf fod, fy Oll, ond gyda Thi,
A chraith rhy faith yw Ddoe i'm calon i.

O tyn...: Opening two lines of a hymn by Hugh Jones of Maesglasau, an ancestral hymn-writer.

Ear-plugs

(a present)

To make a seal of silence in the head
And keep the world at bay; to dam the flood
Of messages that we would have unsaid
And leave the path within awhile untrod
By souls of other men, when we are not
At home for all to call; to wall twice o'er
The entrance to the mind and leave forgot
One hour the urgencies that tap this door:
This is to hide where can alone reside
The meeting of two times; this is to be
A moment where we are; 'tis to abide
Upon a wasted thought unhastedly.
And yet there is a world within this world,
And thinking is with much trapped thinking hurled.

Colditz

To break the law, return and not return,
Saw every vow and promise, and be free
To be alone and sinfully to burn
With but one flame, and shamefully to be
A profligate defrocked of ordered dress
And titles duly preened – to be full naught
And naughtily entwined in one caress –
This were a mighty leap with monsters fraught,
Were it not Thee to clutch and Thee to touch,
My loving, loving Friend, were it not Thine
To walk into a howling desert such
As man braves not without a bread divine:
For though I now may ne'er Thee consecrate
I will Thee love, and for Thy presence wait.

Laughter

And is there med'cine for the universe
Or honey for all ill as sweet as this?
For I have thought, rethought upon a verse
Of ling'ring sweetness in a crystalled bliss
Of calmèd Wisdom felt, of Sound brought on
Again from far away, formed on a day
Long gone, where someone trapped a ray that shone,
And I have heard the healing of the world
In moments spent apart, where hearts alone
Feel all that can be felt, yet e'en the word
Caressed in all its blessing was not known
To jerk the very being with a shock
So great that it could chasmèd cold unlock.

Please, Mr. Postman

There was a song that once the days of youth
Upon a time would hear, where dreams were all
The meaning of a day, and in the truth
That lay in Beauty's sound I still recall
The morrow's pulse in beats of yesterday
When far away were troubles, when to long
For what was not was but to pine away
In pains so sweet that they to bliss belong.
There was a time to love, a time to be
What seemed the fairest dream – there was a light
Within a growing childhood ecstasy
That felt all well, that saw all in the night,
Yet there is time again to hear a song,
And in a sealèd nun a beat yet strong.

In lumine tuo videbimus lumen

(Dad's epitaph)

This is the sky that oft I used to watch
In youth's new heat, in prayer to fervour wed;
This is the height wherein the sight would catch
A glimpse of æons that past dawns had sped
Upon their ancient way – the sight that God
In Man abiding here did also see
When on the Mount of glory He once trod
And on the plain He bade new morsels be:
This is the calmer cov'ring of our days
That will not pass away as soon as they,
And 'tis, perhaps, my Lord, where these soft rays
Of being in us beamed will fade away,
Not in a skelet dust, but in a dream,
A long, long dream, where shone a child's fond gleam.

Consecration

(of hermitage chapel)

Master, 'tis well to be alone with Thee
Here in this place, and here Thy Face to see
Burning with God and shining with the sun
That from the rays of Ancient Days has run.

Master, 'tis well to rest with Thee awhile
Here where we are, and 'neath a prophet's smile
To hear a word once heard by them that came
Past this strange bush where beamed no earth-made flame.

Master, 'tis well to come apart and stay
Here hard by glory dawned at end of day,
And in Thine eyes to see the years arise
In but a word heard by th'engendered skies.

Master, 'tis well to hear a Father's voice
Here in this place sought by the Heavens' choice:
Let us here build a tent where Three may be,
Where in a cloud we may hide mystery.

(On *Abide with me*)

Nunc dimittis

(Dom Siméon)

Dors, dors, ami; dors, père de mon cœur,
Dans ce sommeil attendu, que tes yeux
Ne trouvaient guère ici – mais dors sans peur
De ce grand Au-delà qu'enfin les cieux
A ces paupières scellées, oui, décèlent
A jamais et à jamais, car le soir
De ton cantique, où sans fin se révèlent
Les horizons obscurs, t'a fait tout voir.
Ô bonté inconnue! – Jamais le monde
N'a vu ces yeux fermés, ni ouï le son
De ce cœur arrêté où Dieu seul sonde
Les courants achevés sur ce rayon.
Ô lumière allumée et vite éteinte,
Tiens-moi encore un jour en ton étreinte.

Prepare a talk for me

O Sister, is it come so soon to this,
That thou dost yield and share thy gentle voice,
That thou dost lay a stone and call it his
That is soon here to come? – Is this thy choice,
Sweet unknown heart, or did our part above
Rest settled long ago? – Did many things
At length have oft to happen, ere but love
Unmade of flesh provide a heart with wings?
O cantress too, sing well, for thine old veil
In Tyburn's night a light by Godhead kept,
And thou in maidhood's bloom thy fullest sail
Didst fill with notes so sweet that angels wept
With joy to know that two from very far
Would come to lending organs that they are.

Bleeding statues

Dost thou come, Mother, to this idyl land
To bid it weep awhile, and keep a thought
For th'hour whereon we turn, wherein we stand
Awaiting our return to calmèd Nought?
Do these hard morsels bear a tender heart
That beats beyond the stars, that [illegible] the all
And feels the all of hurting where thou art,
O loving Maid, made here in stone to call?
O Virgin that bore all, call on in blood,
Not in one place but six, and tell a tale
That need not have a voice, nor e'en an end,
For end will all that has begun to fail
On acres blest with grace that Love did send.
For, Italy, thy night is sweet, too sweet,
And 'tis thy stone that knows alone to beat.

Telephone

O silent wire, wherein a fire divine
Moves o'er the earth and, joining star with star,
Marks e'en the depths of man whose heart doth pine
Upon a night to hold what lies afar –
Afar, I say – nay, nay, through thee, wide ear
And voice to oft a voice, full near to where
The list'ning ear doth beat, for two meet here
Where thou alone dost hold two souls not there:
This little trinket hung with hanging charge
Awaiting in the air – alive and well
Where presences see, feel, fall 'neath shocks large,
Too large, too large for but a little bell –
Is one bliss I shall curse, and on our isle
We shall this cord umbilic cut awhile.

Computer

(Please write to me a poem)

How can I write when I know not a soul,
Or e'en a body, though 'tis said 'tis fair,
And how can I through this one part the whole
Of being there devine, as here I stare
Upon a page unwrit, but tapped and pushed
Into an engine's jaw, where none may see
Or feel a face whose chatter may be hushed
At times in old time signs carved daintily?
O child of hastened æons, take a while
To listen to a page, and age to be
Not but a bleep of vision but a style
Of womanhood all felt, where two or three
May gaze upon thy form all naked here
Where rayons of a soul pass without fear.

Holy water

What is a blessing in a molecule,
A cross upon a particle or two
That can, it seems, the fires that demons fuel
Within a sprinkle quench –is this page true,
Castilian Saint, that thou dost quickly pen
And leave to dry o'er centuries to come,
That when the stench of angels foul to men
Is left to reek, weak Grace can Sense benumb?
And is there potion in the darkest night
That can upon a body give repose
When phantoms walk the sky that vapoured light
Unveils to trancèd eyes in opian doze?
Is there a rest not sealed by heavy stone
For him that is with what he is alone?

Donnez-moi le bras, Dom D–

When I recall an eventide of peace
That would at times be ours, when I feel these,
Thy gentle arms, again our pace increase,
As homeward we would walk with measured ease
Lest we be beaten by the Vesper bell
And fail to don aright our cherub wings –
When I behold the sparkle that could tell
A tale to rock the cell with naughty things:
Then, father of my soul, I sometimes sigh
That I'll not love again or be well loved,
And in a placid strength a heart can cry
For but a little move that once much moved.
There was a child in me that loved a man,
And charity well groomed is love too wan.

Gestures

Why do we talk twice-o'er, and heed not once
What is not said? Why does the head not know
How hands to still, and nerves that dance and bounce
To every pulse there sent – as if to show
That we are well at home, that we have heard
Each syllable of sound – can these not stand
Upon a moment's peace, and let a word
Come in and go without a pushing hand?
Untempered South, whose mouthèd truths beat all,
Is soul with soul made louder made to hear,
And is there room in volume for sounds small
Or space in moves so large for moving near?
Is there a way to live, a way to die
With little sound, but little made awry?

Gestures: made by a Sicilian priest-student even on the telephone.

Nazarena

(who died near here 7/2/90, recluded in the
Camaldolese monastery since 21/11/45)

O little one so full of God – so full
Of all that is not seen – nay, never seen
By any but thy Lord, whose gentle pull
Did tug thee, through lured steps, to this vast screen
'Hind which thy pain was hid: thou wast alone,
Unknown, sweet soul, by men, for but thy King
Could gaze into these eyes, and to be known
Was thy one fear in thy strange sheltering.
O word of heavy meaning! I have heard
The clapping of this sound upon a day
Long gone, and yet not wholly gone – this word
Has travelled here before and Yesterday
Still resonates within a syllable
Whose spell made this soft hell invisible.

Holy Saturday

Jerusalem! Jerusalem! This morn
We sing the chant of thy long yesterday
And act in corners four the drama borne
By ages dimmed, for 'tis the Orient ray
That moved Prémontré's dawn, and fossiled bars
Bear music from afar – nay, from the Tomb
Of every tomb to come, wherein the stars
At noon again this day will pierce earth's gloom:
This is the noontide when the fire unlit
Shall come again without the help of man,
And ancient might too bright for human wit
Will calmly strike this wick as no craft can.
For 'tis the ray that blasted Turin's face
That toys with timely sparks from outer space.

No return

O goodness! What is this? What is this light
So tender and so calm, so pure and strong,
That burns upon the world at dead of night
As harlots vigil keep in holding long
The hungering of man – what warmth is this
That has no fear to look into my eyes
And see the man within, nay more, to kiss
'Twixt folds of wimples large a heart that sighs?
O wonder of fond chastity, what flame
Gouged thus the very rust of earth away?
These eyes so blue that but a virgin tame
Did wield, did they but yield a passing ray?
O angels that yet are, and sometimes come,
I have felt burning that shall blast my home.

19/4
(after visit to contemplatives)

Eireann

There is a home from home, an isle whereon
An ancient Eye did look and bid me tread,
A planet far from Earth, where hours move on
At rhythms of their own, for there 'tis said
That e'en all time that is is not enough,
And eyes therein have moments yet to gaze,
To gaze at length, for e'en a land too rough
For high finesse greets yet in softer ways.
And there's a place where there's a space for me
To be a little loved, a little known,
Not in an ant-hill where the millions free
Creep on from glances hid and noses shown,
But in a little corner of the world
That æons missed when they were faster hurled.

End of a book

I thought not that the world would turn this way
When once upon a day this tome did come
From hands that fingered oft what ink could say
Within a list'ning breast – nay, there are some
Faint lines that carry currents strong herein
With shocks not then foreseen when we did sit
Beneath the wingèd engine whose last din
Two worlds brought close awhile would for e'er split.
The hours that called our flight have onward flown
And tapped to thy long tapping, little one,
That word from word hard cleft hast slowly sown
Into a tome thine own where titles shone.
For doctored wast thou by mine ignorance
Of what strange dream upon these lines would dance.

Danger

To be afraid, to be afraid to be
What we were made, to fear to near and hold
What holds a soul, and look, look long, to see
A being all of fire, lest embers cold
Be from safe ashes stirred, and heard to groan
Again from agèd sleep – Aha! to dare
To tread into the virginal unknown
And at a long forbidden sight to stare:
This is a leap where weeps the very dark
Of hid Tomorrow's sin – I'll cross not here
This chasm! Yet did the night of Tyburn mark
In oft a flickered dream what could draw near?
Wast thou then but a wimple and a prayer,
One hid, hid well, in mischief's Eye hid there?

Letter-bomb

O Love! What is this force that fondles me?
O Master! Hold not hard! It is too much
For hominids to feel, for feeling Thee
Is to have held, beheld, a holding such
That naught more holds a spell, that naught on earth
Holds beams enough to warm! I will sign all
Away upon this sheet. A love, 'tis worth
A life of cooling chill – I will here call
The demons out of Hell, and break a vow
That broke all cherub flight, for sighted here
Is Paradise at last, for two can know
A land where three can tremble without fear,
Held in a hold that canons' heavy skill
Shall blast apart no more, though try it will.

L'esame finale

(American military cemetery, Nettuno)

A little moment of a little pain
Before a moment huge, a pain to be
Forgotten in no hour, there where again
No comrade has a friend: eternity
Begins upon a bullet in the sky –
A molecule or two inanimate
That anima will heed, at speed so high
That 'twill the cloud of Myst'ry perforate.
'Twill be – for evermore and evermore –
'Mid earth's revolving days and fading nights
Of memory's short mind, behind this door
That is a little grave, where untraced flights
Flee gadgets highly tuned – 'twill be all told,
The story of a copy-book ne'er old.

The end of the beginning

A place is but a space wherein the world
Revolves upon an axis all its own,
Wherein the corners four are inwards hurled
And much is known that will remain unknown,
But this one corner holds a mighty weight
Of passage into morrows that no eye
Has well espied, and on the stroke of fate,
That tapped our footsteps hither, soft I sigh:
For this, my brethren, is a heavy day
Made of a tear unheard, unformed as yet,
But to be wiped in longing, when the way
Has parted for e'ermore, and this day's set.
For memories will linger for a while
Where this blind eye here shuts away your smile.

The light will write upon tomorrow's page
The moment wherein little words no more
Would come 'tween cups of boreal nectar sage
From urns oft dry outpoured, wherein the store
Of densely laden Knowledge 'twixt the jars
Of denser *butyrum* of peanut hue
Would continents divide, there where the stars
And stripes of culture vast would spread the glue
Of Epicure's delight in *fretta* high
Lest moments be o'erspent – nay, wherein all
Was happy once to be there where no eye
Had time to blink upon a bliss so small.
For we were happy for a little while,
And there can be a sorrow in a smile.

Feast of Saint Romuald

(*Rome* - Hermitage)

O Paradise of peace! O little land
Wherein the world moves not – is this all true,
The vision of the dawn that is at hand,
The sound of this old Angelus I knew
Upon this earth before? This is the day
Whereon I left this isle, this isle of grace,
Nine years of noise ago, and went away
To wand'rings wide, to seek afar Thy Face.
But Thou hast led my feet across the cloud
To Tabor, and Thy tent. I have come home,
And in the light of this Thy Mount the crowd
Shall trample not the soul that long did roam:
O Master, I hear naught but silence vast,
And yet I hear the sound of home at last.

19/6
(having arrived last night)

Mid-summer night's dream

Is this night true, this vision of a time
Once known and felt before - this sound of prayer
Clear-calling in the dark, as footsteps climb
The gravel unto God, on this mount where
There is naught else but He - this odour too
Of wood that sheltered well from all the world,
In alcoves made of Him that here I knew
Before, ere I in haste my treasure hurled...?
O light of this strange night, burn on, burn on,
And glow upon the darkness of this globe.
For though 'tis but a little maiden *nonne*
That holds me safe, I will this chasm probe,
And brave the force of law, for I have found
An ancient beauty in an angel's sound.

So new, and yet so old

Saint Bruno, I ne'er thought that we would meet
Again upon this globe, or that these eyes,
That gazed once on my youth, would see my feet
Walk e'er again 'neath these familiar skies.
O Master of this land wherein is naught
But One alone well known, hold out thy hand
And clear the heavy dark wherein is caught
This path of canons loud where orders stand.
I cannot see ahead, and yet I know
That there is something here in this abyss
Of demon-laden risk, that still doth glow
A little from afar, there where a bliss
Taught once to touch a God, and can again
Teach one long lost here Paradise regain.

The sound of silence

There was a song that used to fill the air
When youth was vibrant yet with many sounds,
And little grooves its harmony would bear
In tunes re-turned with turnings without bounds.
And I did think that there was peace on earth
When all was still save this, thc calmèd wave
Of concord played and caught, for very mirth
Was but of Beauty made, where youth did rave.
But I thought not that I would hear again
This song borne through the mind, not by the pores
Of cables bound, but by the silenced brain
That for a soundless day much sound yet stores.
And I thought not that sound could be like this,
Or that a silence long was softer bliss.

Hermitage

The world sleeps on and on and darkly on,
Yet there is light
And warmth again where hope in youth once shone
Within the night
Of vigils long where song did bathe the air
Of distant quires
That still burn softly there.

O light upon the night where all is heard
In silence pure,
Burn on in seraph cloud there where the Word
In accent sure
Calls from yon bygone age, wherein have burned
These veilèd hearts
That this great song have learned.

O Beauty of a sound wherein is prayer
Upon the dark,
Where far away the dance rocks dimly there
'Neath Satan's mark,
Embalm the calm of virginhood where two
'Mid many wings
Gaze into darkness new.

For home is in a sound and in a light
That leaps the hills
Of Patrick's fire that stilled the roaring night
And this dawn stills
Again with stillness old that holds the dawns
Of many days
Of solitude's lost morns.

O day like any day, yet unlike all
That I beheld,
Come, crack the ice of longing, where doth call
A joy once felt,
And shine upon all time, with no more eve
To darken this
Last truth I can believe.

(Melody: *Lux benigna*)

Notice

(The hermits are praying for you in Silence. They ask that you would respect their Solitude and ring only if really necessary.)

The sound of Sélignac has come afar,
And other sounds have gone: the world knows not
What henceforth will be heard where these words bar
All voices but their own, for here forgot
Will be the talk that need not be, the air
That need be weighed with messages no more,
Save those that drive the day, in this place where
The task is calmly done as once before.
O myriad far away, kept all at bay
By little painted words, gaze on aghast
At what your itch would scratch, and learn to say
Your words to One whose word will be your last.
For there is something here not made of sound,
And this mute dye will cry to hush this ground.

Result

(duly sent to Archbishop)

Aha! A first at last! A little mark
Above the notch of mis'ry – but too late
Are tails here grown and waved, for in the dark
Of hidden days unseen the hustled fate
Of athletes in this race its pace can lose
Before this lengthy moment: nothing more
Is here for me to do, for me to choose
But Thee, my Friend, imprisoned 'hind this door.
O tiny square, there where the æons' King
Looks out at me all hid 'mid atoms strange,
Grant this one other gleam, this little thing
That is within a loaded missive's range:
Bend by a breath the will of him that reads
The plea for that one mark this soul yet needs.

The haircut

From inch to growing inch the hours pull on
These tufts that measure time, and we return
For treatment on this grass, and oft 'twas done
By brethren on the road, who dared to turn
Their academic hands to shearing's craft –
And for a cloistered while to peeling's art,
Where not a twig was spared nor fore nor aft
This globule of a brain that held the heart.
Yet heart nor brain ne'er thought that hours would come
That would be snipped away by little hands
Like this. Nay, there are scenes that puzzle some
That act them on this stage where Time here stands.
The cell I knew before, knew well before,
But in ten years no mirage crossed its door.

The ribbon

(from the Latin breviary)

We are a mighty number when alone,
And on this little ribbon many pass
Between these pages that remain unknown
Save unto some that sat at this great class
Before: I learn the song of ancient time
Oft ticking ere were cogs so finely gauged –
I hear the patter of soft feet that climb
From Yesterday's abyss ere hours thus raged.
I hear, I say, upon the ribbon's length
The turn of days, the ways of many hearts
That into these words moved, there where no strength
But loving's faithful hour its print imparts.
For pages turn where ages turned before
Upon a pattern left on Chronos' shore.

"Watchman, what of the night?"

There is a light upon this ancient mount,
A flame that dawn will find yet burning strong,
There where the sleepy minutes dimly count
The twinkles of the stars, whose vigil long
Perceives the sin of man - Aha! Awake
Are two on this lone height, where evermore
The fire shall burn for One, that time doth take
For Him alone upon this virgin shore.
A flame shall burn tomorrow on this hill
Where naught but darkness pure is seen and known,
And when the rain beats hard this tune will still
Aloft be borne in mingled angel tone.
For here a fire is lit, my sister, where
There was a fair, fair dark two dreams did share.

Dazzling White

(The Transfiguration)

O light, I hear thy touch, a little ray
Not of a flicker trimmed, but of a God
Upon a hill alone with ancient Day
Awaking in the height, here where hath trod
Th'Elijah of the years – here where hath been
The tremble of the Law where fingers moved
Upon the heavy stone, there where was seen
The back of Yahweh's glare by tremors proved.
O Son of Man, I hear a voice not heard
For many a year so well: here passes still
A slightest breath of light that had once stirred
The heart of youth on Meteora's hill.
O Love, I loved Thee well upon this day
But dreamt not that two loves would catch this ray.

6/8
(recalling 6 August, 1972)

You'll never lose me

To know a soul, to know a soul's own soul
And know that 'twill remain - to know that all
The world will turn and pass and that the whole
Of human kind moves on, while yet one call
Will from a wimple come and summon home
There where there is yet ours: that one will be
Upon this hearth of fire where sparks now roam
Amid this cloud of light that two can see
To know, and know within, that there is one
Who will not go away while this world moves,
But that in ageing youth a dying won
By many days of living sacred loves
Will last: at last 'tis knowing I belong
To one alike, if not liked by earth's throng.

Alone

(Was von Anfang war, was wir gehört haben, was wir mit unseren Augen gesehen, was wir geschaut und was unsere Hände angefaßt haben...)

O strange! O trust of Heaven hugely strange
That lets this be, that lets us be alone
'Neath eyes of none, save theirs whose wingèd range
Enfolds our song in peace! O! angel tone
Heard by a veilèd Guest, whose mighty gaze
Knew well the need of twain – upon the hour
Of sacred Godward coming, our twinned days
Are rocked by this thy soft harmonic pow'r.
For I see not the world upon this land
Of shared aloneness vast, I see no friend,
No face but one alone, yet though we stand
Alone upon earth's shore, there to the end
We have a little fire, for two can own
Enough to be for aye on earth alone.

The cell

There are but bricks and mortar on this spot
Of earth trod by a God, there is but wind
In window never filled, for time works not
Too quickly on this isle of labours thinned
By oft a chattered pause; there is not here
Much shelter from the western ocean blast
Nor warmth of hearth where heart to heart may near
Upon a winter's night of loneness vast.
But there is on this ground that will be mine
Hard by the Godhead's fire, a little land
Where I can walk the earth; there is a shrine
'Twixt stone and stone here learning here to stand
Alone for one to be awhile alone
Upon a corner of a God we own.

The prayer-stool

To gaze upon a face that was not seen
And to be seen by none but One alone
Who watches in the dark, and to have been
Naught else but sight wherein was overthrown
The tingle of all sense – to be on earth,
To its last earthly breath, a death to all
That is not made of night, wherein a mirth
Of man's own kind may ne'ermore gently fall –
This is to be here perched upon a beam
That is a fool's long throne, this is to be
A folly in the void, annoyed, 'twould seem,
With time's full fare, yet there I'll promise thee,
Sweet sister, that found time to nail at this,
That every perching shall thee send one bliss.

Εἰρήνη

O joy! There is a joy! There is here joy
Not made of earth, but of a mirth too great
For little hearts like these. No age can cloy
The sparkle of a youth refound, nor late
Is this today in being born, for days
Have waited long for this, and many hours
Must needs have drifted wide ere our two ways
Collided on this shore of distant Pow'rs.
O happiness retrieved! I thought not once
That 'twould e'er come again, nor did the light
Of common day that faintly grew, renounce
The flicker that once glowed, for to this height
Of high Taboric mist I had once gazed,
But had long ceased to hope to be here raised.

Knock

I cannot this believe, I cannot know
How this to take from Thee. I cannot be
At one with truth too great or utter now
A word e'en to my God... O! majesty!
There is yet one Hand there beneath it all,
A Face that glimmers through the trellis twined
By happenings unhappened – nay, a call
This night hath come from dreams long left behind.
O! ecstasy! 'Twill be! This day shall stand
Imprinted on all morrows, and this gaze
Of Godhead from a vast unknown – this Hand
That in a promise deep hath joined two ways
In but a spark of touching – hath clutched hours
To drifting hours in fired æonic pow'rs.

The talk

(given at Knock, but prepared together, over several months)

O Master of the heart, here present still
As I but kneel and gaze, these ways of Thine
Are not of matter made, and yet the Will
Of ages vast has passed through th'atoms' twine,
And in a current's shout the gentle word
Of Godhead too can come, e'en in the voice
Of soft familiar accents often heard
Upon this isle of loneliness' twinned choice.
But there are currents here that I knew not,
And linking waves behaving not too well,
For I have felt a feeling long forgot
To be within a sound, and I can tell
That there is wiring 'tween a soul and soul
Condensed and tensed within another's rôle.

How did you know where I was?

There is a leaking valve in this machine
Of Solitude tight-shut; there is a hole,
A pore, a flaw wherein the armoured screen,
That holds out all the world, holds not the soul
In sealed delight – there is a mighty sound
In whispers in the ear, and near the heart
That would not e'er again by aught be found
There hovers yet a swarm that will not part.
O pull of double pulling! What is this
That fondles yet again what would be gone
From human reach? What is this aching bliss
That in a visage known leaves all undone?
O joy of utter loving! I know not
How friends of yesterday shall be forgot.

A taste of honey

To build upon a desert isle the all
Of earth's heaved industry, to be apart
And 'twixt the commas of the measured call
To incense and to light, to hold the heart
Of all the world's pained song, where labours long
Beat hours from youth and age – to build upon
The rugged soil of Erin, with a throng
Made all of two alone, till light is done:
This is to share the very weight of breath
And know a thought unsaid; this is to do
What many do elsewhere e'en unto death
But with the four same hands, that must undo
The busy industry that can eyes sting,
And bid a monk a maid a soft touch bring.

Present

Upon a lonely hill there is no man
Or voice of human kin, there is here nought
Of fullest nothing made, where nothing can
Be made to make a sound by engines wrought:
There is, I say, no word upon a day
Wherein the skies clap all 'hind distant doors,
Nor comes again a gentle mother's ray
To shine upon a desert land that roars.
But I have found that sound when never made
By Irish eyes and lips, slips quietly
Into the list'ning mind, and I have stayed
Hard by a silent sound unwearily,
For there are presences that I here hold:
One hid, yet there; One hid, yet here of old.

Howling

O! wisdom of fair madness, blown ashore
From this world's mighty sea, where many strive
To beat the current's rage, and wage their war
Against the tempest of the fates that drive
O! wise and fairest ray that was a dream,
That snapped the cords of clinging where no bond
But force of paper held! O! sparkled gleam
That held out 'cross the sea this world beyond
Beyond! There is a place where one can be
A myth of long forgetting, all unsoumd
And loose as carried flotsam, for are we
No more than what we're weighed? Nay, to be bound
But unto one, it is enough for me
For two can shelter well from this great sea.

Completorium

This bell was heard before; this day was done
At this hour oftentimes, and in the eve
There lingers some stray moment once long gone
Yet here again unchanged, and though I grieve
For loitered moments lost, they are not all
A sadness in the heart, for without these
This morrow never thought could not here call.
O Paradise on earth! A home! A home
Where I shall roam no more, but be at one
With Thee, my Guest, my Friend, that in this cell
Dost hide with me till death, for though this sun
Sinks in the stormy West, this gentle bell
Recalls that but an æon is complete,
For this old yesterday I shall repeat.

The face of normal

There is a face that has become the world
Of wonted things; there rings within a sound
That strokes the ear alone, the only word
That can a home ensoul, for home is bound
By little walls so great that none again
Can this domain e'er soil, and where there are
No voices upon earth, lost features wane
And other eyes beam dimly from afar.
O! Oddness of a God that nods at this
Our strange full range of living, where no eye
But His alone half peers... Sweet utter bliss
Of folly doubly bound to cords on high
That pulled a marionette or two confused
To mingling of a soul all purely fused!

Rho im yr hedd a wna im weithio'n dawel

(Canwyd adeg angladd Dad)

O! am yr hedd sydd heddiw'n llifo im
Yn sain y pethau hen, y pethau fu
Fan hyn y ddoe, a ninnau eto'n ddim
Ond rhith ym mreuddwyd maith dy lygaid cu,
Fy Nuw, fy Nghymar cudd – O! am yr hedd
A wn yn awr, yfory wedi hyn!
Yfory ac yfory heb na gwedd
Na chlust na llais ond un dan Rithiau gwyn...
O Grëwr hyn o nos a hyn o ddydd
A ddaw â dim yn ôl i'r dim yr ŷm
Ond golau'r Wawl tu draw, pa awr a fydd
Yn teithio eto'r rhigol lle y bûm
Yn mesur awr ac awr? A fydd parhad
I'r freuddwyd fechan hon a fwriodd had?

Le poêle

Not once, not twice have I shut this small door
That melts the winter ice, yet August skies
Were not then o'er the cell, and what before
Th'All Hallow dawn would bring, I now see rise
In cloud on cloud of scent, each sent to heave
An armour 'gainst the day. – This sound was known
Upon the dark of Sélignac's lone eve
When in stilled youth the fires were slow outblown.
Yet I thought not a morrow such as this
Would one day crisp the dawn, or that this face
Of Silence yawned and shared would one day miss
The count of trespassed years and leap the space
Of yesterday's loud storm, to take one form
Made but of four blue eyes, the winter's norm.

You'll not reach Heaven before me

The records of the Fathers of this land
Wherein we walk alone, the feats of soul
And weakly body tamed, here seem to stand
Before our eyes, that spy again the goal
By Cassian traced, for faced are we this day
By stylites and by dendrites climbing high
And higher still, still higher, till the way
Of no return is found 'neath th'opened sky.
But to be tickled thus, not by the rage
For inches academic, but for hairs
Of goats that itch and rocks and stones that wage
A war with damsel feet – here virtue wears
A Celtic wimpled face, a trace of old
Olympic madness that was passing bold.

Nostrils

To know and to be known, as though one's own
Were in another's breast; to be at rest,
Abiding in a knowledge slowly grown
From signs and signals caught, and to be blest
By blessing of the heart, that needs no more
Than this, the better part to hear again
The sounds that crackled in the night of yore,
And catch the incense that once filled the brain –
This is to trap a molecule of scent
Made of a mem'ry dense; this is to hold
Hard on to wafted hours by shudders sent
Through sensate pores that know the waves of old:
O Master, to know by one nerve the all,
This is to know how vast are holes so small.

Carthusian

There is no way to be what we are not,
And none to be again what yet we are.
O! pain! I cannot leave this land forgot
Or walk upon another! – E'en this star
That in the eve I'd watch from that warm cell
Upon a winter's night, calls from the sky
And bids a hidden tear of hiraeth well
From where a touch too tender came too nigh.
It is too much, the hurt of hurting ne'er
Again with pain well fondled; there is none
Or aught upon this globe to hold me there,
Thy work, sharp nib, that cracked that wall, now done.
Hid Light, shine darkly on. 'Neath altered name
I see in Erin's mist a home the same.

A sleepless night

Alone beneath the stars that bid us sleep,
Alone with none but Thee, my Friend, herein
That dost beside my bed still vigil keep
'Neath this red glow – alone I enter in
To night's long day, where play will trick the stars
To blink their eyes in yesterday's shed light
In vain where neon rules and music mars
The silent melody of ancient night.
O! book upon a bed, it is a while
Since thou didst pupils hold, and I recall
The mischief thou didst wreak when to beguile
The Silignician flame thou didst appal
The gaze of peering masters that bid Out,
For that a soft blue night-line did much shout.

Aware

To know that I'll not be betrayed again
Or left upon a nothing, to believe
That there is in one silent heart a pain
For every other felt, and that to grieve
Is not to grieve alone, where loneliness
Is shared by two that know – to have no fear
To wear a face unmasked, and to caress
With but a gaze of care that all did hear:
This is to rest upon the arms of hope
That dare to gamble all; this is to be
Alone upon a planet where men grope
With sense for sense to touch and eyes to see
All but the hidden parts, for hearts are not
E'er known ere knowing sense be here forgot.

Back

(to the eighth of September)

This dawn has cracked before upon this earth,
And I have heard its sound: I have been here
Before! O! Erin, land of simple mirth
Of ancient moments made, and homesteads dear,
To none of which I walk or talk one hour
From this our silent hearth, – what brought this day
To shine through this dark mist of happ'nings dour
That slammed from door to door on one poor way?
There is a comfort in a little word
Brought by a virgin mother on this morn,
And we shall see again this slumbered world
Of hymnody long dead wake western dawn:
We shall ere long a song of angel quires
Around this chalice host on these home fires.

A little word: Written after Amma came with news from Bishop.

Retrouvé

Ô Sélignac, revenu à l'aurore
À l'aube qui remonte en ce saint jour
Qui m'amena à toi, ce lieu encore
Te porte, et il m'apportera toujours
Le son de ton passage, car cet âge
Est fait de moments connus et vécus
Que nul n'effaçera de cette page
Retrouvée dans un passé survécu.
Aurore faite toute de jeunesse,
J'entends encor ce rythme dont le chant
Fut hier l'écho d'une infinie tristesse
D'humanité aimée la nuit durant.
Ô pointe de l'aurore, encor je sens
Revenir ce seul rêve qui ne ment.

8/9

I cannot give you any more messages

(until you put into practice the ones received)

We shall obey, O Mother, and obey
Until the hurt is great, the fast is strong
And all else faints upon this jagged way
To clouds of fire wherein, 'mid nocturn song,
A Queen all hid is seen, wherein a land
Beyond the veil hard by this vale of tears
Is made 'mid wafted roses soft to stand
While Calm not of this world our cosmos nears.
We have heard Glory's voice upon this hill,
And th'incense in the air was where was not
A meeting as of men, for then the still
And silent list'ning is yet soon forgot,
But here a moment heard has passed us by,
And I have lost my Mother in this sky.

16/9
(Medjugorje)

You'll never know how much I missed you

To know that one is wanted 'neath the sun
That sets upon this isle; to see a smile
Shed by a needing heart, that in but one
Companion on this road hath hoped awhile;
To hear a word oft spoke where words were not
Heard in the desert air, where nothing came
Upon a woman's ear or eye forgot
By all save one that called no more her name –
This is, my God, to touch Thy very heart
That saw me from afar and bid me be
A nothing upon earth, yet there apart
From all, to be the all of one heart's plea
For but one other that would understand
What 'twas upon a lonely land to stand.

17/9
(before the Blessed Sacrament)

Wrenched

When fondness finds a home it can but pain
Too much for hearts like these, and where no more
A word and voice once heard the air again
Bids tremble and tap softly at the door
Of mind and soul entwined in sealèd calm
To bid the dweller of this desert world
Know that the earth has yet a little balm
For thoughts that can be read without a word –
When in one bomb the damnèd angel's work
In fire of clattered rage all age defies
And reawakes a child that long did lurk
'Neath wimples never tamed by manly eyes –
Then there is on this earth a weight of pain
Too great to be here borne alone again.

4/10
(Wales)

Hen ddalen

(o deipysgrif Dad)

O gyfaill cudd, pa ddydd y cawn fwynhau
Y cymun maith lle'r erys oes ac oes
Yn un yfory hir, lle'n aros mae
Y teulu yn yr olaf hun ddi-loes?
O fysedd brau, fu'n brysur yn fan hyn
Ar ddalen wen a'm daliai innau'n fud
Ond huawdl drwy gleisiau du a gwyn
Eich llafur llonydd yn y llafar hud –
Pa fodd y trodd y rhod lle'r erys dim
Ond cof lle bu y corff, ond gosteg maith
Lle bu y llais yn llon a'r geirio'n chwim
Fu'n nyddu doe wrth ddoe drwy'ch tadol waith?
O! farciau hoff, a gloffodd ar eu hynt!
Mi glywaf rywun yma megis cynt.

O deipysgrif: Yn amlwg, fe'i rhoddodd o'r neilltu ac ail-ddechrau.

A kind, familiar sound

(my master's voice)

Saint Bruno, call again, for on this night
I see a ray of hope where gropes the hour
Of darkness born again: a little light
I spy in thy dim smile, and while the pow'r
Of woman is not gone, a man this day
Hath uttered words of newly mitred weight,
With accents known in youth's ecstatic play
As child and father worked at wonders great.
O Altar of first grace! O hands well known!
Will these yet come again and touch my soul
With doubly laden Godhead, that our own
First sharing shall entwine in magic rôle,
Wherein a head, a hand, a head, a hand
Across the centuries at Christ's feet stand?

6/10
(after Bishop Edwin's call)

Offeren Gymraeg

(assisting Fr. Ryan as before)

O little land of hope, O land of song,
O land of mine, mine own 'neath heaven's dome!
I cannot be far from this sound as long
As I in youth had thought, nor can I roam
Tomorrow and tomorrow in this world
Without the eyes I know, the accents fond
That in this vale of tears my soul once heard
In days that weaved of all the deepest bond.
O! Altar on the world, stand high hereon
And let me hold the Lamb where I must be,
There where He gave me flesh, for there is none
Of Erin born that can thee touch as we.
For though the flame is wan, I bear one spark,
And I shall fire thee yet, if giv'n this mark.

Tua'r Gorllewin

Ni allaf fod ymhell o'r erwau hyn
Sy'n suddo dan y don; ni allaf droi
Yn ôl i bell diriogaeth synau syn
Na chlywodd mebyd gynt: ni allaf ffoi
O'r hyn yr ydwyf i, na chau fy nghlyw
I'r dyfnder sydd ry hen, i'r adlais sy'
Yn llefain yn y tir, cans Ti, fy Nuw,
A'm gwnaethost fyth yn rhan o awr a fu.
O Gymru fwyn! Ni allaf droi yn ôl
I sain Yfory pell heb sŵn dy gof,
Ac os bu gwawr rhyw ddoe yn rhyfedd ffôl
Yng ngwynfyd llanc, mi wn mai'n ôl y dof,
Nid at y bryniau hyn sy'n ymbellhau,
Ond at y llefydd ynom sy'n parhau.

29/10
(sailing out of Holyhead)

Fond Abbey, here begins the end

Not once, not twice have I sat in this place
And knelt at this sweet cross, nor is the scent
Of this Thy house, where long Thy tender Face
Gazed hard at me and gentle meanings sent,
A stranger to my brain, but hours untold
Have hither come and gone, and there is not
A gram of dust that mem'ries doth not hold,
For inches often rubbed were not forgot.
O Master, must I go across this world
Without a title worn, or cloth well made,
And be again into a long pain hurled
Where youth grows dim and love's bright fondles fade,
Or canst Thou call somehow across this land
And bid me calmly at some altar stand?

3/11

Kindness, such kindness...

Farewell, fair isle; fade, fade into the past,
And sink beneath the waves of memory
That will lap day and day, until the last
Of dawns dies in the eve of history.
I shall not tread thy shores as one of thine
Again upon this earth; I shall not see
And feel the heat of faces that were mine
To love for but a while upon Time's sea.
O! ripples of short length, the strength of these
Short hours of crossing o'er here crosses all
That might thereon have been, and though this frees
A soul from scandal breakers, something small
Yet lingers in a throat that could have sung
A little yet where yet a goodness clung.

5/11
(sailing out of Dublin)

Waiting

O Silence in the sky, and upon earth
Unheard responses long! What holds the land
Of pilgrim sojourn here for one whose mirth
Lies where no eyes can peer, and where no hand
Can touch but One alone whose touching soft
Hath pulled and pulled thus far? O Guide all hid,
Where wilt thou have me walk, for turning oft
Upon this track, I have not heard Thee bid.
O Darkness of all time, where is the star
That glistened in the dawn, for morn is gone,
And evening by oft falling soon shall mar
The beauty of a dream too oft undone.
O Heaven, move this earth, for I can do
No more where man, it seems, can God undo.

Two letters from Erin

(one from friends with land, the other from a cardinal)

When in the dark there is no mark or sound
To show the way to take; when there is none
That utters aught, and neither ear is found
Nor eye to gaze at all within undone;
When silence is too long where longing lurks
To be somewhere somehow already made
What we were meant to be, and when naught works
In this great engine wherein fate is played:
Then in a little paper there is weight
And sound of calling high; there is in print
Tapped by a red-capped wizard Magic's trait
That of æonic Vision bears some hint.
For though, my Lord, this stillness is too still,
A little hand can hold a Godhead's will.

Prémontré

(A letter from Rome and another from Sant'Antimo)

Saint Norbert, to be 'neath thy mantle yet
And bathed in ancient light – to linger on
A little longer where the ages met
Upon a dot or two not wholly done
But chanted evermore – Ah! Melody!
To hear thee come again across the years
And call me home where wingèd custody
Can hold me bound and safe from freedom's fears:
'Tis to be tugged by one last cord too strong
To be so quickly snipped, for dipped am I
Not in a nocturn rave, but matins long
That have oft sunk 'neath soft Oblivion's sky.
I cannot leave, I cannot leave this land
Of foreshown beauty that becks one last hand.

Letter-opener

(Irish yew, 2000 years old)

The years sapped by this trunk have passed us by
And yet remain to ope the sealèd space
Of slender thinking packed, that th'anguished eye
Will hear vibrate as e'en the distant face
Unseen peers loudly through the silent page,
And strokes or stabs the innards that feel all –
The years, I say, are here, for though we age,
We have the pow'r from hour to hour to call.
And in this gentle slitting of one day
Let yesterday to lie, there is a throng
Of myst'ries hid, for what one page will say
Will in our hist'ry's furrow linger long.
And what we are and will have been will be
Revealed, small tool, nay, for aye sealed by thee.

Genealogy

'Neath every headstone lies a history
And future that ends not where each thin line
Stops on this plotted chart, for mystery
Speaks for a silence vast where passed this fine
And slender thread of Being handed on
By many lying still – nay, one small grave
Holds fast eternity where time has gone
Beneath the billows choked by one last wave.
A scratch or two upon this page we are,
And we must journey on, yet sadness knows
A little gladness in our going far,
For in a trammelled glory something glows.
And I perceive that nothing upon earth
Can matter save one Matter of some worth.

Interpellé

(par les aïeux)

And some there were among these etchèd lines
That stood in pulpits large and beckoned well
To others on the road that fate entwines
With ways and by-ways weaved by peevèd Hell
That stood, I say, where eyes were calmly poised
'Twixt work and work and days and passing days,
And for a little hour a rumour noised
That there were yet in darkness many rays.
These came and went, but did not pass alone
Into that spectred land, but holding still
A myriad in their clutch, 'neath this long stone,
They could their eyelids fasten to none ill.
For in this vale they shepherded much time,
And these old steps I sense their child must climb.

Bouleversé

(par la lettre de S. Antimo)

When at the hour of noon we stand and gaze
At our morn passing by, when we behold
Before our feet the parting of two ways
And from the eve its pattern yet withhold,
And when within we hear a kindred soul
Sigh, "Come this way and rest with us awhile,
For in the written part I see the whole,"
And when 'tis in one "Yea" to end this trial,
Then there is one "Amen" that would but come
Tomorrow for all time, were't not for this
Small particle of earth that is yet home,
For that it holds the faces of old bliss.
And though, my Lord, I catch this incense spell,
Which cloud was sent by Thee I cannot tell.

26/11

Y Saboth olaf

(Last Sabbath in Wales, after latest kind message)

From home to home we wander in this world,
Yet home is not herein, for Paradise
Was not of mortar made, and to be hurled
Into an orbit wide is 'neath the skies
To have no heav'n our own: we were not made
To linger long in loving upon earth,
And where the fondest features slowly fade
We sense not rest where sense alone is mirth.
But I have seen a glimmer on this hill,
Of newness very old, and boldness here
Will crack an ancient wonder: here I will,
In incense dense, of Godhead have no fear,
But rest upon this altar my tired head,
And make my home there where Another bled.

3/12

Reclothed

O Saint of God, that from a Virgin's hand
Didst bear this cloth now giv'n again to one
That roved too long from land to distant land
Without a home beneath this ageing sun,
Wouldst thou here bid me halt and take the pain
Of exile as the heavy cross to be
The part of one alone, nay, and again
This cold well known as all mine ecstasy?
O rapture, wait awhile. I will walk on
A little longer on this well trod way,
For though all sound familiar is now gone,
There is a little glimmer in this day
That dawns upon an altar standing high
Upon an ancient dream now drawing nigh.

14/12

Ange en prière

Ô petit rien voilé par la nuit
De nos regards inachevés, pourquoi
Venir briser encor ce que je suis
Par ce que, seul, tu es, par ce que, toi,
Tu es sans bruit ni son ni gloriole
Qui, pourtant, t'appartient, car seule ici
Avec ton seul Ami, tu es parole
De vérité écoutée et saisie.
O! cœur qui parle et bat pour un seul Cœur!
Tu passeras sans doute en ce demain
Qui portera tes traces, mais, vraie sœur,
Revêtue par les anges, tends la main,
Car j'entre dans la nuit, moi seul, aussi
Et Demain ne te verra plus ici.

29/12
(après Complies)

Completi sunt

Today is but another yesterday
Tomorrow yet to come, and this old year
Was new a while ago, and yet for aye
There is but one wide moment standing here
Upon the which we walk, and there is none
Shall travel other wise, for all the earth
Together plots its course upon this sun
That calls the minutes of our pain and mirth.
O Morrow hugely hid! What bids this night
From its dark entrails come? Where will this hour
Of midnight strike again when one year's light
Fades 'neath the heavy slumber of time's pow'r?
And will this incense sweet yet fill the air
Of this strange call that bids me settle ne'er?

31/12
(after Compline)

Je reste

Ô doigt de Dieu, qui tournes l'univers
Et meus le cœur de l'homme, je te sens
En cette nuit enfin où par ces vers
Le grand Amen se dit, car maintenant
Je sais à Qui je viens, je connais bien
La route ancienne que cet avenir
Contient, car je suis tenu par un lien
Plus fort que ce qui pourrait me tenir.
O! joie d'Amour, de dernier abandon,
De folie qui crie "Tout!" – je veux Te voir
Enfin, grand Dieu, là où l'ultime don
Me place dans la paix d'un nouveau soir
Fait tout de lendemains où Tu seras
Le seul qui dorénavant comptera.

2/1/96

Rome

“Leave not the fold,” they said, “ere thou hast heard
The voice of one more shepherd who can see
With vision better placed; hear one more word
That can in coming save thy destiny
From found’ring well, for something hugely dark
Hangs o’er this whitened way, and in one day
Thou canst nine cent’ries let slip ’yond the mark
Of one life’s last recall with this light play.”
O! pain of double hurt! I cannot be
Upon two parts of earth, or hear this sound
Of echoed history and still be free
To tread again its path where once ’twas found.
O Norbert, look again! I see not well,
For ’tis a day that morrows all will tell.

4/1

Surrender

O! Beauty ever old and ever new
That travels on the air of yesteryear!
I cannot leave again this land I knew
When love was strong, and Song did lull the ear
With meanings of its own – I cannot be
Afar from where I am, for there is more
Within a little space that shelters me
From trudgings long than one strong hingèd door:
There is upon this stone a home where God
Can in my hand be born, there is a place
Hard by a softer light where Brightness trod
A path into my heart – for this Thy Face
I feel upon me beaming in the night,
And I'll not leave this land of loving quite.

14/1

Vixit

Y mae i bapur mud ryw adlais clir,
Ac i lythrennau mân rai creithiau sydd
Yn torri drwy'r hyn ŷm – y mae i'r gwir
Ryw allu dros yr awr a'r oriau fydd
Yn treiddio 'fory'r rhod, a nod y graith
Sydd ar y ddalen hon a erys dro
Ar wyneb haul a lloer boreau maith
Na welant wedd yr hun sydd dan y gro.
Yfory ni fydd inc a ddaw yn ôl
Ag odl o'r tir pell lle'r erys oll
Yn ddistaw a di-sill, a synau ffôl
Ein synied am a fydd i ti sy'ngholl,
Ein cyfaill cu, a fuost am fer awr
Yn llewyrch brau o wenau Blaen y Wawr.

Vixit: Rev. Emrys Edwards, a neighbour and friend, used to correspond with me in verse.

Caterina

O fun yn un â Duw, yn fwy na dyn,
Yn ddynes yn dy gorff ond yn dy ddawn
Yn fugail i'r pen fugail mawr ei hun,
Ac yn dy gnawd yn newydd gnawd i'r Iawn –
A gofi heddiw'r cerrig henaidd hyn
Llc safodd gynt dy droed, a'r oed lle bu
I fintai gref at wyry wen yn syn
Ymsymud heb na sain na murmur su?
A glywi heno, chwaer, yn nef y nef
Yr hen gyfaredd hon sy'n dod yn ôl
O garreg ac o garreg lle bu llef
Sawl pell golledig sant yn nefol ffôl
Yn llenwi gofod gwag â seiniau mân,
Yn llenwi gofod oes â hen, hen gân?

Un être te manque, et tout est dépeuplé

To think and think again on what has been,
And to recall an hour when all was lost;
To see again the eyes that are not seen,
And to behold one moment that all tossed;
To utter oft within the breast soft sounds
That by none here below will e'er be heard,
And to be bound by sorrow that no bounds
Can hold or soften by an answered word:
This is, my friend, hence silent to the end
Of these our parted days – this is to be
A sadness that no morrow now can mend,
For that the sight of one it shall not see:
The face of one that held awhile the world
Was on a day to darkened days e'er hurled.

Reçu

O! sorrow evermore and nevermore
To be alone here held – I am where love
Can in a fond embrace as once before
My calmèd soul enlace: I hear above
This altar where we'll meet a gentle breeze
All of a Presence made, I hear again
Upon the tranquil night what no eye sees,
For in one word is heard an end of pain.
O Master, I will come and Thee ere long
Hold o'er the world 'mid echoes of fair tune,
And in the morrows of this ancient song
I will hold well the rays of this last boon,
For love has called me here, and I shall stay
Until one fondness lost has passed away.

22/1

Enough

A cell is but a wall or two of stone
Of nothing made, with nothing weighed but air,
And there is neither face nor voice to own
The little man that can but ponder there,
And yet there can be in an emptiness
A sound that oft was found upon this shore
Of seconds that we tread, where blessedness
Laps for a while our land as once of yore.
For I can hear, my Lord, within this place
A rhythm that I know, and I can tell
The meaning in the look of this Thy Face
That I see not, for man sees not here well,
Yet there is here enough for one to be
A salvaged morsel of eternity.

"Dñs Hugo fecit nos fieri omnis Alpha et Omega Anno Dñi MCCXVIII"

Ring out again upon these Tuscan hills
Your brazen song of measured tempo known
By oft a passing ear, with sound that stills
The moving of all time, for in this stone
That hears again the echo that your call
Draws hourly from our breasts, there lingers yet
A wonder of long finding: something small
In this your poisèd stroke holds hours long set.
O! souls that flew this way and glided on
To where this sun now sets – O! westward clan,
That lies in skelet form where days have gone
Beneath this tapping of the tune of Man –
Await a little on this patient shore
Of minutes that have lapped this land before.

Cassé

O maid and mother, known to one alone,
Who once had heard thy song and known thy voice
Upon a lonely land that two did own
A little while, what was this unthought choice
That chose all time asunder to be held
And to be made to be what it shall be
For ever, ever more – what thus withheld
What could have calmly been all history?
O little one now lost, now tossed away,
Why didst thou pause not at the morrow's door
That in a mighty moment on a day
In one strong strident second all things bore?
O! woman kind, so kind and cruel to man,
You wave a wand that no known Godhead can.

Yesterday

When I recall the voice that called my name
Across the Hibern wind, when I behold
Again upon the mem'ry's screen the dame
That o'er my hermit's dream all sway did hold,
And when I hear the cantress in the air
The praise of glory 'mid the incense bring
To Godhead's list'ning ears – when I tread there
Yet never there again shall ought e'er sing –
Then in this Tuscan cell, 'neath hooded thought
All of an echo made, I hear too much
For one shaved head to bear, for I hear nought
Of what the figment's image would fain clutch
A little while again, were it not so,
The pow'r of yesterday its way to go.

For ever

O! peace! O! peace! To know that we have found
A corner of the cosmos wherein all
May safely lie at rest, where naught but sound
Of gentle yestertone may henceforth fall
Upon the troubled ear, where we may be
Alone for love alone where all the world
May hear no more our voice or ever see
The heart that beats herein upon a word –
To know, O Logic hid, that Thou art there,
Amid the maddest course that brought us here,
And to feel tingle something in the air
Of incense dense where Godhead travels near:
This is to rest awhile upon a Breast
Whereon the æons yawned lie 'yond the West.

30/1

In petram inaccessam mihi deduc me

O joy! I shall yet hold Thee in my hand
Upon this ancient stone where others felt
The passing of their God: I shall there stand
Where souls have stood before and angels knelt
At veilèd Mystery – I see the light
Of Tabor in this night, for this one word
Of manhood made is weighed with Godhead's might,
And in one chrismic sound I have all heard.
O Master of this astral path we tread,
I hear, I hear the voice that never was
By mortals caught, and here my little head
I bow to Thy great blessing: this day has
A ray of touch electric hither sent,
And o'er a sound the heavy cosmos bent.

24/2

O joy: after Fr. Prior's return from Siena, with the news from the Archbishop about Profession and Ordination.